# INTERPRETING THE NEW TESTAMENT

## A Practical Guide

Daniel J. Harrington, S.J.

A Michael Glazier Book
THE LITURGICAL PRESS
Collegeville, Minnesota

A Michael Glazier Book
*published by*
THE LITURGICAL PRESS



Cover: The Avignon Fresco, National Gallery of Ireland.


Printed in the United States of America.

13 14 15 16 17 18 19 20

**Library of Congress Cataloging-in-Publication Data**

Harrington, Daniel J.
Interpreting the New Testament : a practical guide / Daniel J. Harrington.
p. cm. — (New Testament message ; 1)
Reprint. Previously published: Wilmington, Del. : M. Glazier, 1979.
"A Michael Glazier book."
Includes bibliographical references.
ISBN 0-8146-5124-0
1. Bible. N.T.—Hermeneutics. 2. Bible. N.T.—Criticism, interpretation, etc. I. Title. II. Series: New Testament message ; v. 1.
BS2331.H37 1990
220.6'01—dc20 90-42839
CIP

# Contents

# EDITORS' PREFACE

*New Testament Message* is a commentary series designed to bring the best of biblical scholarship to a wide audience. Anyone who is sensitive to the mood of the church today is aware of a deep craving for the Word of God. This interest in reading and praying the scriptures is not confined to a religious elite. The desire to strengthen one's faith and to mature in prayer has brought Christians of all types and all ages to discover the beauty of the biblical message. Our age has also been heir to an avalanche of biblical scholarship. Recent archaeological finds, new manuscript evidence, and the increasing volume of specialized studies on the Bible have made possible a much more profound penetration of the biblical message. But the flood of information and its technical nature keeps much of this scholarship out of the hands of the Christian who is eager to learn but is not a specialist. *New Testament Message* is a response to this need.

The subtitle of the series is significant: "A Biblical-Theological Commentary." Each volume in the series, while drawing on up-to-date scholarship, concentrates on bringing to the fore in understandable terms the specific message of each biblical author. The essay-format (rather than a word-by-word commentary) helps the reader savor the beauty and power of the biblical message and, at the same time, understand the sensitive task of responsible biblical interpretation.

A distinctive feature of the series is the amount of space given to the "neglected" New Testament writings, such as Colossians, James, Jude, the Pastoral Letters, the Letters of Peter and John. These briefer biblical books make a significant but often overlooked contribution to the richness of the New Testament. By assigning larger than normal coverage to these books, the series hopes to give these parts of Scripture the attention they deserve.

Because *New Testament Message* is aimed at the entire English speaking world, it is a collaborative effort of international proportions. The twenty-two contributors represent biblical scholarship in North America, Britain, Ireland and Australia. Each of the contributors is a recognized expert in his or her field, has published widely, and has been chosen because of a proven ability to communicate at a popular level. And, while all of the contributors are Roman Catholic, their work is addressed to the Christian community as a whole. The New Testament is the patrimony of all Christians. It is the hope of all concerned with this series that it will bring a fuller appreciation of God's saving Word to his people.

Wilfrid Harrington, O.P.
Donald Senior, C.P.

# INTRODUCTION

THIS INTRODUCTION to New Testament exegesis aims to help readers of the New Testament Message series by explaining to them in a simple and brief way the basic literary methods used in studying the New Testament today. It is a beginner's book, designed to make explicit some of the procedures now instinctively used by the commentators who have indeed had formal exegetical training and probably no longer need to make explicit the methods that they apply. In short, this is a modest attempt at supplying the readers of the New Testament Message series with some formal exegetical training. It touches only in passing on theological matters (since the commentaries will handle them) and historical matters (since a separate volume by Sean Freyne will treat these). Rather, this volume explains how the methods used in the study of literature can also be effectively and fruitfully employed in *reading* the New Testament. Throughout the presentation the emphasis is on the logic of the methods being described and on the value of their application to the Scriptures.

Each chapter (with the exception of the one on form criticism) consists of an exposition of a method, two examples of how the method can be applied to specific texts, and a list of five to ten bibliographic suggestions. (1) The expositions of the methods focus on the questions to be asked of the biblical text and on what can be legitimately expected as answers to these questions. Usually some indications are provided about the origin and development of the methods and about the broader theological and historical problems raised by them. The choice of methods to be explained is somewhat conventional, with only slight attention paid to the so-called "new methods" such as liberation exegesis, psychoanalytic exegesis, and structuralism. This is a book for "beginners," and the methods described here are basic and well tested, whereas the "new methods" are very complicated and are still in the process of development. (2) In most chapters there are two sample applications of the method under consideration to texts—usually one from the Gospels and one from the Epistles. Since the New Testament Message series is based on the Revised Standard Version (RSV), I have generally cited the texts according to that translation. Though the Synoptic Gospels receive a somewhat larger share of space than the other parts of the New Testament do, an effort has been made to spread the examples out. The exegesis in these examples does not represent my private fantasies or pet theories. I have tried to pick out interesting cases and to present in my own words what I and what many other exegetes have said. Not all interpreters, however, will agree with the understanding of this or that text. If the reader of this book agrees with my presentations, I will be pleased. But if the reader disagrees and is stimulated to find convincing reasons for holding a different interpretation, then I will be even more pleased. (3) To each chapter I have appended a brief bibliography of books and articles published in English. The character of the bibliographies varies according to the subject matter. For example, in the chapter on textual criticism the emphasis is on recent discussions of methodology, while in the case of literary parallels the stress is on the source materials themselves. I have usually cited the books according to their American publishers, but many of them are also available in British editions. The title will give the reader an idea of what is contained in the book or article and provide some initiation into the areas of current debate. Those who wish more bibliographic information about the New Testament field should consult Joseph A. Fitzmyer's *Introductory Bibliography for the Study of Scripture* (Subsidia Biblica 3; rev. ed.;

Rome: Biblical Institute Press, 1981) and *New Testament Abstracts*, ed. Daniel J. Harrington (Cambridge, MA: Weston School of Theology). See also Joseph A. Fitzmyer's *An Introductory Bibliography for the Study of Scripture* (Subsidia Biblica 3; Rome: Biblical Institute Press, 1981), and Erasmus Hort's *The Bible Book* (New York: Crossroad, 1983).

At the time when the Catholic Church is looking back on the documents of the Second Vatican Council and evaluating the extent to which they have been implemented, this book can be seen as a partial response to the third chapter in the Dogmatic Constitution on Divine Revelation. Paragraph 12 of that document insists on the divine origin of Scripture but insists just as strongly that God speaks through human beings in human fashion. It urges exegetes to look for the meaning that the sacred writer in a specific situation and culture expressed through the medium of a contemporary literary form. It emphasizes that due attention must be paid both to the customary and characteristic patterns of perception, speech, and narrative which prevailed at the age of the sacred writers and to the conventions which the people of this time followed in their dealings with one another. I hope that this modest book may be of some help in translating these directives into the life of the church and in helping more Christians to enter into the exciting task of biblical exegesis.

Daniel J. Harrington, S.J.

# I. LITERARY CRITICISM IN GENERAL

## *A. The New Testament Literature*

WE FREQUENTLY speak of the New Testament as if it were a single book with a beginning, middle, and end. But anyone who takes the time and effort to read straight through the New Testament soon realizes that it is a collection of quite varied writings unified by the belief that Jesus of Nazareth marks the most decisive intervention of God within human history. The New Testament begins with four rather long documents—the Gospels of Matthew, Mark, Luke, and John—that tell the story of Jesus up to and including his death and resurrection. The first three Gospels seem quite similar in vocabulary, literary style, and tone, and so they are frequently called the "Synoptic Gospels" because they share a "common vision" of Jesus. The Fourth Gospel with its journeys to and from Jerusalem and its long discourses delivered by Jesus paints a very different portrait of Jesus. The Acts of the Apostles tells the story of the early church from the ascension of Jesus to Paul's arrival in Rome and appears to have been written by the same person who composed the Gospel of Luke (see Acts 1:1-4).

Next in the sequence of New Testament books there come the thirteen epistles traditionally attributed to the apostle Paul. They are not arranged according to their date of composition or according to their theological importance. Rather, two basic external principles are at work in the presentation of the Pauline letters. They are

# 1. LITERARY CRITICISM IN GENERAL

## *A. The New Testament Literature*

WE FREQUENTLY speak of *the* New Testament as if it were a single book with a beginning, middle, and end. But anyone who takes the time and effort to read straight through the New Testament soon realizes that it is a collection of quite varied writings unified by the belief that Jesus of Nazareth marks the most decisive intervention of God within human history. The New Testament begins with four rather long documents—the Gospels of Matthew, Mark, Luke, and John—that tell the story of Jesus up to and including his death and resurrection. The first three Gospels seem quite similar in vocabulary, literary style, and tone, and so they are frequently called the "Synoptic Gospels" because they share a "common vision" of Jesus. The Fourth Gospel with its journeys to and from Jerusalem and its long discourses delivered by Jesus paints a very different portrait of Jesus. The Acts of the Apostles tells the story of the early church from the ascension of Jesus to Paul's arrival in Rome and appears to have been written by the same person who composed the Gospel of Luke (see Acts 1:1-4).

Next in the sequence of New Testament books there come the thirteen epistles traditionally attributed to the apostle Paul. They are not arranged according to their date of composition or according to their theological importance. Rather, two basic external principles are at work in the presentation of the Pauline letters. They are grouped first according to whether they are addressed to communities (Romans through 2 Thessalonians) or to individuals (1 Timothy through Philemon). Then within this twofold division they are presented according to their material length. So the epistles addressed to communities are in descending order of length: Romans, 1 Corinthians, 2 Corinthians, Galatians, Ephesians, Philippians, Colossians, 1 Thessalonians, and 2 Thessalonians. Then the four epistles to individuals appear also in descending order of length: 1 Timothy, 2 Timothy, Titus, and Philemon. After the epistle to the Hebrews, which has only a vague connection with the Pauline letters (see Heb 13:22-25), the group of writings called the Catholic Epistles occurs in this order: James, 1 Peter, 2 Peter, 1 John, 2 John, 3 John, and Jude. The word "catholic" means "universal," and it may have originally made the point that these epistles are addressed "to all the churches" as it was understood in the East or that they were recognized as authoritative "by all the churches" as it was understood in the West. The last book in the collection that we call the New Testament is the book of Revelation or the Apocalypse. Though it contains brief "letters" to the seven churches of Asia Minor (see Rev 1:4—3:22), the book is really the account of a vision about the past, present, and future that was granted by God to its author. Four Gospels, one Acts, twenty-one Epistles, and one Apocalypse—these twenty-seven documents of diverse origin, authorship and theological perspective constitute the collection of New Testament books that we call the "canon."

The writings that make up the New Testament are first and foremost pieces of literature. Surely these books are not the cultivated and aesthetically pleasing literary productions that might be constructed in keeping with the general rules laid down by Aristotle or a modern literary critic. Rather, these books belong to a popular kind of literature that came out of a religious community's experience—a community that from the beginning seems to have been more interested in oral communication than in written documents and more concerned with witness than with logical persuasion or demonstration. Nevertheless, the New Testament contains the literary expression of the primitive church's life and faith and should be approached initially as literature. Because the New Testament consists of twenty-seven pieces of literature, we have the obligation to try to understand those writings by the methods of approach and the standards that have proved successful in the study of other literary works as well. Literary criticism means putting to the New Testament books the kind of questions that people in departments of literature ask—questions about the ability of language to express thought, about the significance of literary structure for meaning, and about the relationship of content to literary form. They are not really very complicated questions. When one gets into the habit of asking them of a text, the ability to answer them for oneself and on one's own grows concurrently.

Suppose that you are confronted with a brief passage from the Bible. You may have heard it or read it often before this time, but now you wish to go deeper, to penetrate to the meaning of the text, to appreciate it more fully than ever before. How do you go about it? What questions are to be asked? How can you listen to the text and so gain new insight into something that you may consider to be very important? At its most elementary level literary criticism is first of all interested in the words of the text and the images and symbols that they evoke. Words (and the phrases and sentences that they form) are the raw material of any piece of literature, and the intelligent reader must have some confidence about the accuracy of the text and about the meaning conveyed by the various parts of the text. So the first question to be asked and answered in the elementary kind of literary-critical analysis envisioned here is this: What words, images, and symbols appear? This fundamental question must not be ignored, even if the reader must sometimes consult a dictionary, a commentary, or some other reference work to answer it adequately. To proceed without an initial understanding of the text's raw material (its words) is to court a final misunderstanding. It requires some intellectual humility to admit that one does not really understand the words of a text and some courage to take the necessary steps to remedy one's lack of understanding.

The second question concerns the overall movement of the text: What characters appear, and what are their relationships? Obviously this question is most relevant to narratives in which personal figures appear and interact; but even in the case of a piece of expository prose, it can be helpful to get straight precisely who is saying what about whom or what and how the parts are related. The third question is also concerned with the overall movement of the text: What is the progress of thought? To use the word "thought" here runs the risk of suggesting that literary criticism is really only interested in the ideas or messages conveyed in texts. Nothing could be further from the truth! This third question simply demands that the reader, having first understood the words and having become aware of the characters or units of thought involved, then become conscious of the flow of the text. This is done not simply to abstract out "the basic point" but rather to increase one's awareness of the artistic devices used in the process of communication.

The notion of artistic communication becomes clearer in the fourth and fifth questions involved in elementary literary criticism: What literary form does the text have? How does the form contribute to expressing the content? In everyday speech we use a variety of verbal and written forms to communicate with others. We tell stories, ask questions, provide information, make small talk, and so on. The very form we choose often communicates on a preverbal level much of what we wish to convey in the end. For example, if I want a piece of information from someone considered likely to possess it, the easiest way to proceed is to use the literary form most likely to elicit it: I ask a question. What time is it? Where are you going? Will you come this evening? I may vary or add to the basic pattern depending on who is addressed ("Sir," "Pardon me," "John," etc.), but the direct question is the most effective means of getting whatever information I want and need. Similarly, the questions about the literary form of the written text demand that I be aware of the variety of forms available to a biblical writer and that I make an effort to see how the literary form and the content of the text are in mutual relationship.

These five major concerns of elementary literary criticism—the words, the characters, the story or thought line, the literary form, the relation between form and content—can help the reader to enter the world of a written text and understand it more thoroughly than ever before. They are probably familiar operations that have been explained and practiced in undergraduate or even high-school courses in English literature. They can be applied to Sacred Scripture too. Elementary literary criticism can heighten our understanding and appreciation of a novel or a sonnet or a play, and there is every good reason to suppose that it can enrich our reading of the New Testament also. In the pages that follow I would like to lead the reader through two brief and probably familiar texts—the so-called parable of the good Samaritan from Lk 10:30-35 and the doxology in Rom 11:33-36. I will address to each passage the five questions of elementary literary criticism, pausing at those points at which something especially significant may emerge. These examples are meant to illustrate the practice of literary criticism, not to say the last word about the interpretation of either text.

## *B. Examples of Literary Criticism*

1. *Luke 10:30-35:* The term "good Samaritan" has long been a familiar description of a stranger who helps a person in a crisis or a time of real need. The expression comes from

a parable found in Luke's Gospel that is used to illustrate Jesus' teaching about loving one's neighbor. Jesus is asked: "And who is my neighbor?" The Lukan narrative continues in this manner:

> [30]Jesus replied, "A man was going down from Jerusalem to Jericho, and he fell among robbers, who stripped him and beat him, and departed, leaving him half-dead. [31]Now by chance a priest was going down that road; and when he saw him he passed by on the other side. [32]So likewise a levite, when he came to the place and saw him, passed by on the other side. [33]But a Samaritan, as he journeyed, came to where he was; and when he saw him, he had compassion, [34]and went to him and bound up his wounds, pouring on oil and wine; then he set him on his own beast and brought him to an inn, and took care of him. [35]And the next day he took out two denarii and gave them to the innkeeper, saying, 'Take care of him; and whatever more you spend, I will repay you when I come back.'"

The story can be approached in several ways (e.g., its place in the Gospel of Luke, its possible origin in Jesus' preaching), but here it is cited to illustrate the value of putting to a New Testament text the basic questions of literary criticism.

What words in the text are foreign or not readily intelligible? Today's reader would probably not know that the road "down from Jerusalem to Jericho" involves a journey of about twenty-five miles proceeding northeast from the religious and political capital of Israel to an ancient city revived in the time of Herod the Great. The word "down' refers to the fact that the way from Jerusalem to Jericho is a winding mountain road descending from 2,250 feet above sea level to 900 feet below sea level. The road with all its twists and turns was a favorite haunt for robbers. The social status of the three passers-by may also need explanation. The complexities of the origin of the Israelite priesthood need not concern us here. It is enough to say that priests and levites held their offices by their birth into appropriate families and that a system had developed according to which various priests and levites participated in the Temple worship according to a regular yearly schedule. The story of Lk 10:30-35 may assume that the priest and the levite were returning from Jerusalem after having taken their turns in the rites at the Temple. There is some remote possibility that their refusal to minister to the wounded man was due to their fear of ritual impurity brought about by contact with a corpse. On the other hand, the Samaritan came from the area of Palestine situated between Galilee and Judea. Suspected of being a "non-Jew" by the Judeans, the Samaritan plays the role of the foreigner over against the priest and the levite. A hint of "anticlerical" humor seems to be present in the story. The "two denarii" mentioned in Lk 10:35 as the Samaritan's contribution to the care of the wounded may also present a puzzle. Fortunately the note in the older editions of the RSV ("the denarius was worth about twenty cents") has been replaced by a more informative and intelligible note ("the denarius was a day's wage for a laborer") presumably based on Mt 20:9 where the denarius is understood to be the daily wage for an unskilled worker. This kind of information about the geographical relationship between Jerusalem and Jericho, the social status of the passers-by, and the value of the denarius can be readily found in the annotated editions of the Bible or in any reliable commentary. It is necessary for understanding the dynamics of the story.

What characters appear, and what are their relationships? The three passers-by have already been described. The man who was robbed and beaten appears at the very beginning of the story, and the innkeeper is addressed at the end. The one character that remains on stage during the whole narrative is the man who was robbed and beaten. Left for dead by the robbers, he was passed by a priest and by a levite. But the Samaritan had compassion on him, dressed his wounds, and handed him over to the care of the innkeeper. The man left for dead is the one principle of continuity running through the story, and every other character has some kind of relationship with him.

What is the progress of thought? Recognition of the central role of the man left for dead vis-à-vis the other characters makes the answer to the third literary-critical question fairly easy. In v.30 the scene is set: The traveller has been beaten, robbed, and left for dead. Vv.31-34 describe the three passers-by and contrast the noninvolvement of the priest (v.31) and the levite (v.32) with the compassionate involvement of the Samaritan (vv.33-34). In the last verse (v.35) the crisis is resolved, and provision has been made for the wounded man.

What literary form does the text have? Obviously it is a narrative as opposed to a poem or a proverb or a logical argument. It is in fact a model of good storytelling. No extraneous details like the names of characters, their physical descriptions, etc., are allowed to distract the listeners from the central line of the story. The use of the first two passers-by sets up a pattern of expectations (noninvolvement on the part of the priest and the levite) without boring the listeners and prepares for the contrast to be sprung in the part about the Samaritan. The stress is on the third passer-by whose behavior is very different from that of the priest and levite. The story proposes to recount an incident that is intelligible to the audience (being robbed on the Jericho road) but is not part of their everyday experience and so is of some special interest to them. To ask whether this robbery actually occurred at a particular time and place is to miss the "typical" element of the story. This individual case clearly points beyond itself toward something of general importance. The story of the good Samaritan is usually called a parable; that is, a brief narrative about an interesting individual case that points toward something very important for human existence.

How does the form contribute to expressing the content?

Before answering that question, the content of the parable should be clarified. The storyline of the parable indicates that the wounded man is the central character. We are to identify first of all with him, put ourselves beside him in his crisis, and answer along with him the question, "Who is my neighbor?" The answer is that my neighbor is the one who does me a kindness in my hour of need, even if he happens to be a Samaritan. In thinking about neighborliness, we must be prepared to abandon our prejudices and our presuppositions. This interpretation of the parable is confirmed by the framework in which it is placed in Lk 10:29 ("But he, desiring to justify himself, said to Jesus, 'And who is my neighbor?'") and 10:36-37a ("'Which of these three, do you think, proved neighbor to the man who fell among the robbers?' He said, 'The one who showed mercy on him.'").

The point could be made in a variety of literary forms, but the parable appears to be an especially effective means of communicating it. There is an instinctive fondness in human beings for a well-told story. The parable draws the reader into the narrative; and when the conclusion is sprung, a personal response is demanded ("go and do likewise"). Personal identification with the wounded man enables us to answer the question, "Who is my neighbor?" Having recognized the rightness of the Samaritan's compassion, we then are urged to identify with him and follow his example. The parable allows the audience to think for itself and to draw its own conclusion. It allows for much more personal response and appropriation than the more didactic and direct literary forms do.

(2) *Romans 11:33-36:* At the end of his long and twisting meditation on the significance of Israel and the church in the history of salvation, Paul summarizes his position: "a hardening has come upon part of Israel, until the full number of the Gentiles come in and so all Israel will be saved (11:25-26)." After a brief explanation of how God is now guiding all people toward salvation, Paul expresses his

admiration for the divine plan with an emotional outpouring of praise:

> [33]O the depth of the riches and wisdom and knowledge of God! How unsearchable are his judgments and how inscrutable his ways!
>
> [34]"For who has known the mind of the Lord,
> or who has been his counselor?"
> [35]"Or who has given a gift to him that he might be repaid?"
> [36]For from him and through him and to him are all things.
> To him be glory forever. Amen.

The text singles out certain praiseworthy attributes of God—riches, wisdom, and knowledge. The language is general and somewhat abstract, but nothing in the passage needs much explanation. The cast of characters is equally simple. Paul does the praising, and the object of his praise is God. Many of the phrases in the passage have a liturgical ring to them, and perhaps we are meant to get a sense of communal worship too. The language and characters in Rom 11:33-36 are clear and demand little commentary.

The progress of thought and literary structure of the text, however, make it a particularly interesting case. It begins with two exclamations praising (1) the depth of the riches and wisdom and knowledge of God and (2) the unsearchable nature of his judgments and the inscrutable character of his ways. Then there are three questions based upon Old Testament texts (see Is 40:13 and Job 41:11) asking for the identify of anyone who (1) has known the mind of God, (2) served as his adviser, or (3) given him a gift that demands repayment. Finally God is praised as the origin, agent, and goal of all created things. A liturgical tag concludes the passage: "To him be glory for ever. Amen." Attention to the kinds of sentences—two exclamations, three questions, a concluding formula—found in the text obviously increases our understanding of it. But there is even more to the structure of Rom 11:33-36. The first exclamation praises the riches, wisdom, and knowledge of God. The three questions take up these three attributes of God in reverse order: knowledge ("who has known the mind of the Lord?"), wisdom ("who has been his counselor?"), and riches ("who has given a gift to him that he might be repaid?"). In other words, between the first exclamation and the three questions there is an interlocking descending (ABC) and ascending (C′B′A′) pattern. This kind of formal structural pattern is not unusual in the New Testament Epistles, and awareness of its presence in a passage like Rom 11:33-36 adds to our appreciation of Paul's literary skill.

What literary form does the passage have? Rom 11:33-36 is generally described as a doxology. In fact, the word "glory" in the liturgical conclusion is the translation of the Greek *doxa*. A doxology is literally a "word of glory." In a doxology the distinctive features of a person (here, God) are praised. The language is general, and the tone is enthusiastic. An "eternity formula" ("to him be glory for ever") concludes the doxology. The use of a doxology naturally evokes the mood of a community worship service.

Why did Paul use a doxology at this point in the epistle to the Romans? How did the doxology form contribute to the content that Paul wished to communicate in the epistle? The meditation on Israel and the church in Romans 9—11, far from being a digression in the plan of the epistle, is Paul's attempt to show that God's righteousness can be discerned even in the present hardening of heart by some in Israel. The position enunciated in Rom 11:25-26 comes as the climax of a difficult and sometimes strained argument. It is as if Paul said: "I finally have it clear!" The present hardening of heart that has come upon part of Israel is only temporary until the Gentiles can become part of God's people. Paul has made his point in vv.25-26 and backed it up with scriptural and other considerations in vv.27-32. But his enthusiasm is still not spent, and so the doxology is an especially appropriate vehicle for him to give expression to his feelings of wonder and admiration at the divine plan. Moreover, as the conclusion to a sophisticated and difficult argument spread over three long chapters of the epistle, the doxology serves to remind the reader that the topic under discussion touches the core of humanity's relationship to God and is no mere debate about empty words.

## *C. Literary Expression and Theological Content*

These two examples illustrate the questions that a literary critic operating at a very basic level would put to a text and the answers that can be reasonably expected from such questioning. But the literary criticism of the New Testament does not stop at this elementary level. In fact, the literary criticism of the New Testament encompasses the whole complex of methods that have been developed over the centuries and that represent the subject matter of this book. Textual criticism explores the relationships between the various manuscripts of the New Testament and attempts to determine the original wording of a text. Attention to the renderings found in modern English translations of the Bible can make us more sensitive to the range of meanings of individual words and raises the problem about effectively communicating the meaning of an ancient text. Word study explores the history of biblical terms and motifs in the hope of understanding better this or that particular instance. Source criticism tries to say what materials the authors had at their disposal in the process of producing their own literary creations. Form criticism surveys the range of literary forms available to an author and tries to determine what the history of these forms can tell us about developments within early Christianity. Historical criticism is concerned with the event behind the text and explores what can and cannot be said about a past occurrence on the basis of a literary witness. Redaction criticism is interested in the editorial achievements of the final author and the community for which he wrote. The study of parallels to a biblical text tells us what was "in the air" when the New Testament was written. The history of interpretation brings to bear on a text the linguistic skills and theological insights of the great patristic, medieval, Reformation, and modern interpreters. Hermeneutics examines what a text can mean for us today and how it can be a source of consolation or challenge in the church's preaching and prayer. All these different approaches to the New Testament text comprise the discipline of literary criticism taken in the broad sense of that term. They are not ends in themselves but are designed to contribute to the reader's appreciation of the text taken as a whole. Used piecemeal, they can easily degenerate into sheer pedantry. Used wisely and with an eye toward grasping the meaning of the whole text, they can increase our comprehension and love of the Scriptures.

The discussion of literary criticism in this chapter began with a general survey of the types of writings found in the collection that we call the New Testament: Gospels, Acts, Epistles, and Apocalypse. In the course of the discussion of literary criticism there was a good deal of emphasis on the mutual relationship between form and content. The interaction of form and content is perhaps nowhere more evident than in the larger literary genres of the New Testament. Each of the larger literary genres (Gospels, Acts, Epistles, Apocalypse) belongs to a recognizable literary category (biography, history, letter, revelation account), but everyone of them has a special twist precisely because of the Christ-event that it proclaims.

The Gospels tell about the life of Jesus. They are not treatises in systematic theology or encyclopedia articles giving only the facts of Jesus' life and achievements or scientific biographies produced according to the standards of modern historiography. Rather, they retell the foundational story of what Christians believe to be God's decisive encounter with humanity in Jesus of Nazareth. Written by believers for believers, the Gospels invite us to enter into the teachings and deeds of the one who is confessed to be the risen Lord present within the Christian community. The Gospels may look like biographies, but the peculiar character of Christian faith makes these documents into something slightly different. If history is understood as the recording of the story of the past, then the Acts of the Apostles looks like a history book. Acts is the story of how the church reached its identity and spread out all over the world from Jerusalem to Rome. The word "story" in that description is important. Acts is a delightful combination of historical facts, Christian traditions, and original insights all in the service of Luke's conviction that after the ascension of Jesus the Holy Spirit was guiding the church and making it prosper.

The New Testament Epistles have the outward appearance of letters. Many of them contain the usual epistolary greeting (sender, recipient, greeting), the thanksgiving, the body of the letter, and the conclusion. At least the genuine Pauline letters (see Appendix One) are occasional documents written for a particular group (the Romans, the Corinthians) in a particular situation, and yet they are not simply private letters having no relevance beyond their original setting. On the other hand, the Pauline letters are far from being general treatises on the nature of Christ or the essence of the church. No, they are a peculiar blend of the particular-occasional and the core gospel and thus illustrate how the gospel of Christ achieves incarnational depth in the particulars of the human situation.

Finally, the Apocalypse is the report of a vision or revelation that uses strange images and symbols, concentrates on the end of history, and views everything as under God's control. But the Apocalypse of the New Testament differs from its Jewish analogues primarily because of its conviction that Jesus Christ has inaugurated or already begun the final age. In all these cases, form and content go hand in hand.

## *Bibliography: Literary Criticism*

R. Alter and F. Kermode (eds.), *The Literary Guide to the Bible* (Cambridge, MA: Harvard University Press, 1987).

W.A. Beardslee, *Literary Criticism of the New Testament* (Guides to Biblical Scholarship, New Testament Series; Philadelphia: Fortress, 1970).

N. Frye, *The Great Code. The Bible and Literature* (New York—London: Harcourt Brace Jovanovich, 1982).

J.H. Gottcent, *The Bible as Literature. A Selective Bibliography* (Boston: Hall, 1979).

G.A. Kennedy, *New Testament Interpretation through Rhetorical Criticism* (Chapel Hill, NC—London: University of North Carolina, 1984).

N.R. Petersen, *Literary Criticism for New Testament Critics* (Guides to Biblical Scholarship, New Testament Series; Philadelphia, Fortress, 1978).

D.O. Via, *Kerygma and Comedy in the New Testament. A Structuralist Approach to Hermeneutic* (Philadelphia: Fortress, 1975).

R. Wellek and A. Warren, *Theory of Literature* (3rd ed.; New York: Harcourt, Brace, and World, 1962).

A.N. Wilder, *The Language of the Gospel. Early Christian Rhetoric* (New York—Evanston, IL: Harper & Row, 1964).

A.N. Wilder, *Theopoetic. Theology and the Religious Imagination* (Philadelphia: Fortress, 1976).

# 2. TEXTUAL CRITICISM

## *A. Principles of Textual Criticism*

WE HAVE no manuscript of a biblical book written directly by its author. The texts that we do possess derive from the originals (or autographs) through a number of intermediary copies. And with each copying, the possibility and indeed the likelihood of mistakes or alterations entering into the manuscript tradition grow. Textual criticism seeks to produce a text as close to the original as is humanly possible. New Testament textual criticism is obviously a very technical enterprise involving the personal inspection of manuscripts written in Greek and other ancient languages. A detailed discussion of it in a simple introduction to the methods of exegesis would be out of place. It will be sufficient if the reader grasps that New Testament textual critics must weigh the external evidence of the manuscripts, explain rationally whatever variant readings occur, and take into account the context, language, and style of the document in arriving at their decision about the form of the original text.

The first question facing the textual critic is this: Are there ancient variant readings? Perhaps the major obstacle encountered in New Testament textual criticism stems from an embarrassment of riches. There is too much material available for quick and simple decisions. In establishing the text of a classical or a patristic writing an editor generally has a limited number of manuscripts (say ten or twenty) which usually can be neatly arranged in a diagram (called a stemma) showing how one manuscript depends directly or indirectly on another. But the New Testament was too popular and perhaps too revered to allow for such simple exactitude. One inventory (now several years old) counted 85 papyri, 268 majuscules, 2,792 minuscules, and 2,193 lectionaries.

The *papyri* are fragmentary manuscripts from the second and third centuries. Their great antiquity is balanced by their often poor physical condition. The *majuscules* are Greek manuscripts written entirely in capital letters and coming from the fourth to the tenth centuries. The most important majuscules are the Vatican manuscript customarily designated by the symbol "B" from the early fourth century and containing the Old Testament and most of the New Testament in Greek, the Sinai manuscript designated by the Hebrew letter *aleph* that comes from the middle of the fourth century and contains the Old Testament as well as the New Testament and some of the Apostolic Fathers in Greek, the Alexandrian manuscript designated by the letter "A" and from the fifth century, and the Codex Bezae designated by the letter "D" and assigned to the fifth or sixth centuries. The *minuscule* manuscripts distinguish between large and small letters and represent a style of writing that began to dominate by the eleventh century. The *lectionaries* contain selections from biblical texts used in liturgical contexts.

Besides the wealth of Greek materials available to the New Testament textual critic there are also important ancient translations into Syriac, Coptic, Latin, Armenian, Slavonic, Gothic, etc. Some of these versions may depend upon a Greek text earlier than any presently existing Greek manuscript, and so they can be very important in arriving at a text-critical decision. The writings of the Fathers of the church need also to be taken into account. The Fathers were primarily interpreters of the biblical tradition, and they can provide precious indications about the form of the biblical text in certain locales from a time when we have no direct manuscript evidence.

Some external features of the Greek manuscripts make the text-critical task even more complicated. The earliest texts (the papyri and the majuscules) left no spaces between individual words and contained no accents, breathing marks, or punctuation. The division of the New Testament into chapters came into fashion only around A.D. 1200, and the division of the chapters into verses was carried out in the middle of the sixteenth century. Furthermore, as the sacred texts were copied and recopied by scribes whose memories and familiarity with other biblical manuscripts could hardly be turned off at will, the New Testament writings suffered textual contamination. For example, a scribe instead of merely copying from one good Greek manuscript, may have taken readings from the several texts to which he had access and thus produced a new entity on his own. This process of contamination makes practically impossible the construction of a neat diagram of relationships between New Testament manuscripts. The best that can be done is to work out a theory of "local texts" according to which various manuscripts are grouped together according to geographical designations: Alexandrian (represented by the Vatican and Sinai manuscripts), Western (Codex Bezae), Caesarean, and Byzantine (the "Alexandrian" manuscript). Up through the middle of the nineteenth century the printed editions of the Greek New Testament were based on a Byzantine-type of manuscript, and so also were the translations based upon them (for example, the King James Version). Gradually the Alexandrian text was recognized as purer and more authentic, and it is the basis for the modern scholarly editions and for translations like the Revised Standard Version.

All this information about the New Testament text has been presented as necessary background to the question: Are there ancient variant readings? A variant reading is an instance in which two or more manuscripts differ regarding the form of a text. A modern editor is forced to choose between readings by printing one as part of the text and relegating the other (or others) to the foot of the page.

Given the quantity and variety of witnesses and the complicating factors connected with the transmission of the New Testament, one can expect a fairly large number of ancient variant readings. The textual critic's first step is simply to describe the situation; that is, the nature of the variants, the number of witnesses for the different readings, and the age and quality of the manuscripts in which they appear. The word "quality" is very important because the manuscript evidence must be weighed rather than merely counted. For example, imagine two copyists at work in the second century A.D. The first scribe copied correctly, but the second made an error. The first manuscript was copied thereafter only two or three times, and the only copy still existing was made in the fifteenth century. Nevertheless, that single late manuscript is correct over against the thousands of existing copies made from the erroneous second manuscript. A possibility like this takes textual criticism out of the realm of sheer counting and into the arena of the rational consideration of the existing evidence.

The mention of rational consideration leads to the second question facing the textual critic: What can be explained away as unconscious or conscious alterations? Anyone with an experience of handwriting or typewriting knows how unconscious mistakes can occur, and most of the same kinds of errors that we make are to be found in the ancient manuscripts of the New Testament. The major mechanical errors are writing the same word twice (dittography), omitting letters or words (haplography), exchanging one letter for another because of similar form or sound, misunderstanding a marginal note or a correction, and misinterpreting an abbreviation. But conscious deviations can occur also as when scribes "corrected" the grammar or the style of the text, assimilated the form of an Old Testament quotation or allusion to the wording that was most familiar to them, brought verbal consistency to two parallel New Testament texts, and imposed their brand of theological orthodoxy upon the biblical text. In deciding to accept one reading as part of the original text and to relegate the others to the foot of the page, the editor must be prepared to explain how all the rejected readings could have developed from the one original reading. In other words, the editor must call upon the usual sources of unconscious or conscious error in the effort to show how the rejected readings developed from the reading judged as original.

There is some limited validity to the general rules that the shorter readings and the more difficult readings are to be preferred. The preference for the shorter reading is based on the assumption that, where no convincing mechanical or conscious explanation is forthcoming, one must reckon with the usual human tendency to expand upon what had already been written. If the aim of textual criticism is to determine what the original author said, then following the shorter readings will probably help in achieving that goal in the absence of any other rational explanation. The preference for the more difficult readings is also based on a common human tendency—the tendency to simplify what seems complicated or foreign. Of course, sometimes a reading can be so difficult that the only reasonable conclusion is that it is erroneous. But if a reading seems on the surface to present a problem but on mature consideration does make sense, one should be very cautious about rejecting it for the apparently easier version. These are only general rules, and in any individual case the "longer" or the "smoother" reading may well be correct.

All the talk about unconscious and conscious errors and about shorter and more difficult readings may leave one asking: How reliable is the text of the New Testament? In fact, the text of the New Testament has been preserved with a greater degree of certainty than can be claimed for almost any other book from the ancient world. There are some good reasons for this claim: the abundant evidence of the Greek manuscripts and the early translations, the continuity of the textual tradition from the earliest times of the church to the present, the general carefulness of the scribes in preserving the text, the continued use of the text in the church's life and worship, and the development of textual criticism as a scientific discipline.

Having considered how ancient variant readings can arise in a New Testament text, we now can turn to the third question: What reading is demanded by the context, language, and style of the document? Arriving at a correct decision about the original form of a text is not a purely external procedure divorced from literary appreciation. In choosing one reading over another the textual critic must be sensitive to the phrasing and to the thought patterns of the individual author. A reading in Matthew's Gospel or the letter to the Romans that flatly contradicts what can be known about the literary practices of Matthew or Paul should be rejected as inauthentic. A reading that confuses or interrupts the logic of a passage is suspect too. These points are obvious, but I state them here to correct the false impression that textual criticism is a purely mechanical operation requiring little or no attention to the literary character of the document being edited. Indeed it would be entirely appropriate to discuss textual criticism only after the other exegetical methods had been treated. The fact is that intelligent textual criticism presupposes a thorough and informed understanding of all aspects of the text.

## *B. Examples of Textual Criticism*

1. *Matthew 6:33:* The RSV reads: "But seek first *his kingdom* and his righteousness, and all these things shall be yours as well." This translation reflects the text of the earliest Greek manuscripts, but several fairly important though later manuscripts have the phrase "kingdom of God" or "kingdom of heaven" rather than "his kingdom." The weight of the manuscript tradition favors the short reading, and it is difficult to understand why "of God" or "of heaven" would have been deleted on mechanical or conscious grounds if it were part of the original text. The matter could be considered settled in favor of "his kingdom" except for a peculiar feature of Matthew's literary style. In an overwhelming number of instances where the word "kingdom" occurs in Matthew's Gospel it is accompanied

by the phrase "of God" or "of heaven." So one is forced to choose between a reading reflecting the weight of the external evidence ("his kingdom") or one consistent with Matthean style ("kingdom of God" or "kingdom of heaven"). In this kind of case the textual critic necessarily deals in probabilities, but the comparative lateness of the manuscript evidence for "of God" and "of heaven" and the fact that Matthew does sometimes use "kingdom" without a modifier (see 8:12; 13:38; 24:7,14) suggest that the earliest version of Mt 6:33 read simply, "his kingdom."

2. *1 John 5:8:* The text of 1 John 5:8 in the RSV (5:7-8 in the Greek) reads: "There are three witnesses, the Spirit, the water, and the blood; and these three agree." Though this is an accurate translation of what is found in the overwhelming majority of Greek manuscripts, four late Greek texts from between the eleventh and sixteenth centuries have a longer version: "There are three witnesses, [in heaven, the Father, the Word, and the Holy Spirit; and these three agree. And there are three witnesses on earth,] the Spirit, the water, and the blood; and these three agree." The additional material is the so-called Johannine comma. A decree of the Holy Office in 1897 decided (since rescinded) in favor of the long text as authentic but few (if any) modern textual critics and exegetes agree. Why is the short text almost universally regarded as reflecting what was contained in the original text of 1 John and the long text rejected?

The most obvious argument against the authenticity of the long text is its very poor attestation in the manuscript tradition. It is absent from every Greek manuscript except four relatively late ones and from all the ancient translations except the Latin. In fact it is not even present in the earliest versions of the Latin Bible, and only from the sixth century onward was it at all frequent in the Latin biblical tradition. None of the Greek Fathers of the church quoted it, and they would hardly have ignored it in their controversies about the Trinity if they had known it as part of Scripture. So from the viewpoint of external witnesses the long text is very suspect.

How can the presence of the so-called Johannine comma in the later tradition of the Latin Bible and in the few Greek manuscripts be explained? The long text probably originated as an allegorical commentary on the three "witnesses" cited in the text in terms of the persons of the Trinity. A copyist or a later reader may have inserted a note to this effect in the margin of a biblical manuscript as an attempt to clarify the meaning of a difficult text. Then another copyist came along and mistakenly inserted the marginal note into the body of the text. The earliest instance of the note's being quoted as part of the epistle is in a late fourth-century Latin treatise called *Liber Apologeticus*, but by the fifth and sixth centuries the Latin Fathers of the church cited it as if it belonged to the biblical text. Yet virtually all modern commentators agree that the insertion only confuses an already difficult passage. 1 John 5:6-12 does have a trinitarian dimension, but "water and blood" refers to Jesus in 5:6 and may echo the tradition of blood and water flowing from the side of the crucified Jesus in Jn 19:34-35. Therefore the Johannine comma is suspect textually on three counts: (1) It is poorly attested in the Greek manuscript tradition and in the ancient translations. (2) It may be reasonably explained as originating from a marginal note later inserted into the Latin Bible and subsequently into a few Greek manuscripts. (3) It interrupts and confuses an already difficult passage. For further details, see B. M. Metzger, *A Textual Commentary on the Greek New Testament* (London—New York: United Bible Societies, 1971) pp. 18, 716-718.

## *Bibliography: Textual Criticism*

K. Aland et al. (eds.), *The Greek New Testament* (3rd rev. ed.; New York—Stuttgart: United Bible Societies, 1983).

K. and B. Aland, *The Text of the New Testament* (Grand Rapids: Eerdmans, 1987).

E.J. Epp, "The Eclectic Method in New Testament Textual Criticism: Solution or Symptom?" *Harvard Theological Review* 69 (1976) 211-57.

E.J. Epp, "The Twentieth Century Interlude in New Testament Textual Criticism," *Journal of Biblical Literature* 93 (1974) 386-414.

J. Finegan, *Encountering New Testament Manuscripts: A Working Introduction to Textual Criticism* (Grand Rapids: Eerdmans, 1974).

J.H. Greenlee, *Scribes, Scrolls, and Scripture. A Student's Guide to New Testament Textual Criticism* (Grand Rapids: Eerdmans, 1985).

P. Maas, *Textual Criticism* (tr. B. Flower; Oxford: Oxford University Press, 1958).

B.M. Metzger, *The Canon of the New Testament. Its Origin, Development, and Significance* (Oxford: Clarendon Press, 1988).

B.M. Metzger, *The Early Versions of the New Testament. Their Origin, Transmission, and Limitations* (Oxford: Clarendon Press, 1977).

B.M. Metzger, *The Text of the New Testament. Its Transmission, Corruption, and Restoration* (2nd ed.; New York/Oxford: Oxford University Press, 1968).

B.M. Metzger, *A Textual Commentary on the Greek New Testament. A Companion Volume to the United Bible Societies' Greek New Testament (third edition)* (London/ New York: United Bible Societies, 1971).

C.H. Roberts and T.C. Skeat, *The Birth of the Codex* (New York—London: Oxford University Press, 1983).

V. Taylor, *The Text of the New Testament. A Short Introduction* (New York: St. Martin's Press, 1961).

# 3. TRANSLATIONS

## *A. Six Modern English Translations*

WHY ARE THERE so many new English translations of the Bible? Which one is the best? Such questions come immediately to the mind of anyone today who browses through the religion section of a large bookstore. For many years Protestants got along with the King James Version (1611) or its British (1881-1885) and American (1901) revisions, and Catholics made do with the Douay translation (1609-10; rev. ed., 1749). But since World War II English-speakers have been presented with a large number of new translations made by committees of prestigious biblical scholars or by learned individuals (for example, R. A. Knox and J. B. Phillips).

What factors made these new translations necessary? Advances in textual criticism showed that the Greek manuscript tradition on which the King James Version was based (the so-called "Textus Receptus" representing the Byzantine group of manuscripts) was not the most ancient and reliable. The Douay Bible was translated from the Latin Vulgate and so was a step removed from the original Greek. Furthermore, nonbiblical Greek texts of all kinds had become available, thereby enriching our knowledge of the Greek language and the meaning of its words. Finally, the English language had developed considerably over the centuries. Some words in the earlier translations became old-fashioned or even unintelligible, and others had their meaning changed significantly. Meanwhile, English had become as close to an international language as exists in the world today, but the English Bible remained encased in an apparently peculiar and outmoded (however beautiful) dialect. All these factors provided the inspiration that has produced our new English translations of the Bible.

This discussion of modern English translations of the New Testament is limited to the six most widely circulated versions published since 1946. They all were prepared by committees of academics and church officials for use in private study and (in some cases) in public worship. All are good and reliable translations, though their purposes and philosophies of translation differ widely. They are described here in the chronological order of the publication of their New Testament sections.

The *Revised Standard Version* (1946; second edition, 1971) is an authorized revision of the American Standard Version published in 1901, which was in turn a revision of the King James Version published in 1611. Unlike the other modern versions, the RSV is a "traditional" version in that it deliberately seeks to preserve all that is best in the English Bible as it has been known and used through the years. The RSV makes no claim to be a new translation in "the language of today," though obviously it aims at a more modern kind of English than the KJV provides. Originally prepared under American Protestant auspices, it was granted an *imprimatur* by Cardinal Richard Cushing of Boston in 1965 and its revision committee over the years has included several prominent Catholic biblical scholars.

The *New English Bible* (1961) marked a genuine departure in the history of English translations. A team of British Protestant biblical scholars under the general direction of C. H. Dodd set out to produce "a faithful rendering of the best available Greek text into the current speech of our time." What represents the departure is the phrase "the current speech of our time." The NEB adopts the translation philosophy of dynamic equivalence: "We have conceived our task to be that of understanding the original as precisely as we could (using all available aids), and then saying again in our own native idiom what we believed the author to be saying in his." Though urged not to stray over the boundary of translation into the area of paraphrase, the NEB translators were encouraged to replace Greek constructions and idioms by those of contemporary English. Whereas the RSV is a literal translation frequently content to reflect the ambiguity of the original texts, the NEB is concerned to say what the biblical writers meant in so far as this can be determined.

The translation philosophy of dynamic equivalence underlies two translations published in 1966. The *Good News Bible* or *Today's English Version* as it is sometimes called was translated and published by the United Bible Societies for use throughout the world by people for whom English is either the mother tongue or an acquired language. This new translation seeks to state clearly and accurately the meaning of the original texts in words and forms that are widely accepted by people who use English as a means of communication. It attempts to set forth the biblical content and message in today's standard, everyday, and natural form of English. The *Jerusalem Bible* was prepared by British Catholic scholars under the direction of Alexander Jones. Its introductions and notes are direct translations from the French *La Bible de Jérusalem*, though these were revised and brought up to date in some places. The initial translations of the biblical books were usually made from the Hebrew or Greek and simultaneously compared with the French when questions of variant readings or interpretations arose. The JB had a twofold objective: to translate the Bible into the language we use today and to provide notes that are neither sectarian nor superficial. The JB is somewhat more cautious or restrained than the NEB and the GNB/TEV about accepting the philosophy of dynamic equivalence. On the one hand, the JB is written in the language of today and studiously avoids the "biblical English" dictated by tradition. On the other hand, the JB refuses to allow its translators to substitute modern images for old ones or to impose their own literary styles on the original texts.[1]

The *New American Bible* (1970) and the *New International Version* (1973) represent something of a return to the philosophy of formal correspondence represented by the RSV. The NAB is the work of members of the Catholic Biblical Association of America, though not all the collaborators were Catholics. It seeks to be "suitable for liturgical use, private reading, and study." The goal of formal correspondence is summarized in these words from the preface: ". . . the temptation to improve overladen sentences by the consolidation or elimination of multiplied adjectives, or the simplification of clumsy hendiadys, has been resisted here. For the most part, rhetorically ineffective words and phrases are retained in this translation in some form, even when it is clear that a Western contemporary writer would never have employed them."[2] The NIV was prepared by an international group of Protestant scholars "committed to the full authority and complete trustworthiness of the Scriptures." Their first concern was the accuracy of the translation and its fidelity to the thought of the New Testament writers, though the translators recognize that faithful communication of the meaning of the original text demands frequent modification in sentence structure and constant regard for the contextual meanings of words.

These six modern English translations represent the combined efforts of distinguished scholars and literary stylists. They are published in a variety of formats and have provided the base text for several series of commentaries. Instead of discussing them abstractly, we might profit more by studying their various renderings of two specific passages—Mk 1:14-15 and Gal 3:19-20. The aim of these sample discussions is to provide some personal acquaintance with the six translations. The Greek text presupposed by the translations, the difficult decisions encountered by translators in each passage, and the general philosophy of translation operative in each version will be

[1] A thoroughly revised edition (NJB) under the direction of Henry Wansborough appeared in 1985.

[2] A thoroughly revised edition of the NAB was published in 1987.

the major areas of concern. In the process the reader will become familiar with the most important questions to be asked when using and evaluating an English translation of the Scriptures.

### *B. Examples of Modern English Translations*

1. *Mark 1:14-15:* The first part of the first chapter in Mark's Gospel is a kind of introduction or prologue to the whole story of Jesus. After announcing the subject matter in v.1, the passage describes the relationship between Jesus and John the Baptist (vv.2-8), tells about the baptism of Jesus by John (vv.9-11) and the testing of Jesus in the wilderness (vv.12-13), and summarizes the content of Jesus' preaching (vv.14-15). My own very literal translation of the Greek text of Mk 1:14-15 reads in this way: "And after John was delivered up, Jesus came into Galilee, preaching the gospel of God, and saying that the time has been fulfilled and the kingdom of God has drawn near. Repent, and believe in the gospel." This is the kind of translation that students in beginning Greek would be expected to give back to a teacher with the intention of proving that they had really understood the Greek text. There is an English word for practically every Greek word in the text. The images present in the Greek roots have been retained as far as is possible. No real effort at good English style is made. Such a rigidly literal translation would probably seem a bit foreign to someone unfamiliar with New Testament Greek and might well end up in obscuring the meaning of the biblical text.

The six translations that we are considering here attempt both to be faithful to the original Greek text and to express the content of the text in correct and intelligible English. These are their renderings of Mk 1:14-15:

*RSV:*

> Now after John was arrested, Jesus came into Galilee, preaching the gospel of God, and saying, "The time is

> fulfilled, and the kingdom of God is at hand; repent and believe in the gospel."

*NEB:*

> After John had been arrested, Jesus came into Galilee proclaiming the Gospel of God: "The time has come; the kingdom of God is upon you; repent, and believe the Gospel."

*GNB/TEV:*

> After John had been put in prison, Jesus went to Galilee and preached the Good News from God. "The right time has come," he said, "and the kingdom of God is near! Turn away from your sins and believe the Good News!"

*JB:*

> After John had been arrested, Jesus went into Galilee. There he proclaimed the Good News from God. "The time has come," he said, "and the kingdom of God is close at hand. Repent, and believe the Good News."

*NAB:*

> After John's arrest, Jesus appeared in Galilee proclaiming the good news of God: "This is the time of fulfillment. The reign of God is at hand. Reform your lives and believe in the gospel."

*NIV:*

> After John was put in prison, Jesus went into Galilee, proclaiming the good news of God. "The time has come," he said. "The kingdom of God is near. Repent and believe the good news."

Are all of these translations based on the same Greek text? Not exactly, though the six do agree in the really substantial parts of the passage. All the translations except the RSV begin with the word "after" and clearly depend upon the Greek *kai meta* (literally "and after"). The phrase "now after" in the RSV probably reflects the Greek variant *meta de* and has been chosen because the Greek particle *de* indicates important turning points in Mk 7:24; 10:32; and 14:1. Furthermore, at the beginning of v. 15 most of the translations have the phrase "and saying" (RSV) or "he said," but the NEB and NAB lack this phrase. It is hard to know whether these translations are following those Greek manuscripts that omit the words *kai legōn* ("and saying") or they are simply being economical in their use of words and omitting what seems unnecessary. At any rate, apart from these two very minor points, all six translations reflect the same Greek text.

What kind of decisions did the translators have to make about the meaning of the text? My literal translation has no quotation marks within the text, but all the other versions place quotation marks before "the time" and after "the gospel." The use of the second person plural "you" in the verbs of the second sentence of the quotation confirms that this part of the passage is direct address. Why in my translation did I use the word "that" and omit the quotation marks? The answer is simple. The Greek manuscripts had no convention for indicating direct address by way of punctuation marks and introduced a quotation by the word "that" (*hoti*). Here the translators are correctly substituting the English convention of quotation marks for the Greek convention of introducing a quotation with the word "that" (*hoti*).

Comparison of the six translations reveals that Mk 1:14-15 involves far more important interpretive decisions than whether or not to use quotation marks. Most of the versions contain the expression "the gospel of God" (RSV, NEB) or "the good news of God" (NAB, NIV), but "the good news *from* God" occurs in the GNB/TEV and JB. Is the gospel "of God" or "from God?" The word "God" is in the genitive case in Greek and could be either objective ("the gospel about God") or subjective ("the gospel from God"). The translations that use the word "of" avoid making a clearcut decision and so reflect the ambiguity of the original text, while the GNB/TEV and JB leave no doubt that "of God" is to be taken as a subjective genitive. Another translation problem involves the word "kingdom." The NAB stands alone in rendering the word *basileia* as "reign" presumably to avoid the spatial and static sense of "kingdom," but the other translators apparently felt that such a strategy was unnecessary. There is a surprising unanimity in understanding the verb that accompanies "the kingdom of God": "is at hand" (RSV, NAB), "is near" (GNB/TEV, NIV), "is close at hand" (JB), and "is upon you" (NEB). The translations agree that the kingdom of God is very close but deny that it has already arrived. Other points of translation could be raised here ("is fulfilled" versus "has come" and "believe in" versus "believe"), but enough has been said to demonstrate that intelligible translation frequently demands hard decisions about the meaning of a text.

What philosophies of translation are behind these versions of Mk 1:14-15? The text is a fairly straightforward summary of Jesus' preaching, and the differences between the translations are not too obvious. But if my translation is taken as a standard for literalness, the RSV emerges as the most literal text ("and saying" and "is fulfilled") while the GNB/TEV is least literal ("put in prison," "Good News from God," "the right time," "turn away from your sins"). The other translations are somewhere in between these two extremes.

Has anything been lost in the translations? My translation begins by describing John the Baptist as having been "delivered up" whereas the others speak of his having been arrested (RSV, JB, NAB, NEB) or put in prison (GNB/TEV, NIV). The translations correctly explain what had happened to John, but they may be obscuring an important point. The Greek term for "delivered up" (*paradidonai*) is used frequently by Mark in connection with Jesus' passion and death (see Mk 3:19; 9:31; 10:33; 14:10,11,18,21,41,

42,44; 15:1,10,15) to suggest that all this took place in accordance with the divine plan. The "delivering up" of Jesus is God's will. By using the same word to describe the fate of John the Baptist, the Evangelist insinuates that there is a parallelism or a close relationship between the destiny of John and that of Jesus. None of the translations makes this apparent, but they probably should have done so.

2. *Galatians 3:19-20:* Paul wrote to the Galatians in the mid-fifties of the first century A.D. in order to provide guidance for them in dealing with a serious religious crisis. After Paul had founded the church at Galatia (in the middle of present-day Turkey) and had moved on in carrying out his missionary activities, some Christians at Galatia became infatuated with Judaism and wished to establish a kind of Jewish Christianity that Paul judged to be a perversion of the true gospel (see Gal 1:7). In chapter 3 of his epistle Paul tried to prove that Christians accepting his gospel are the true children of Abraham (see 3:29) and that those who even suggest that observance of the Mosaic Law could bring about right relationship with God or justification preach a false gospel. If (as Paul maintained) the Law cannot bring about right relationship with God, then what was the purpose of that Law? Note that Paul was talking specifically about the Mosaic Law, and not about law in general. If the Law given to Moses could not guarantee salvation, what reason did God have in revealing it at all? That is the question to which Gal 3:19-20 tries to provide at least a partial answer.

My own excessively literal translation of Gal 3:19-20 is this:

> Why therefore the law? For the sake of transgressions it was added until there might come the seed to which it was promised, ordered through angels, by the hand of an intermediary. Now the intermediary is not of one, but God is one.

The six translations offer these versions of the same text.

*RSV:*

Why then the law? It was added because of transgressions, till the offspring should come to whom the promise had been made; and it was ordained by angels through an intermediary. Now an intermediary implies more than one; but God is one.

*NEB:*

Then what of the law? It was added to make wrongdoing a legal offence. It was a temporary measure pending the arrival of the 'issue' to whom the promise was made. It was promulgated through angels, and there was an intermediary; but an intermediary is not needed for one party acting alone, and God is one.

*GNB/TEV:*

What, then, was the purpose of the Law? It was added in order to show what wrongdoing is, and it was meant to last until the coming of Abraham's descendant, to whom the promise was made. The Law was handed down by angels, with a man acting as a go-between. But a go-between is not needed when only one person is involved; and God is one.

*JB:*

What then was the purpose of adding the Law? This was done to specify crimes, until the posterity came to whom the promise was addressed. The Law was promulgated by angels, assisted by an intermediary. Now there can only be an intermediary between two parties, yet God is one.

*NAB:*

What is the relevance of the law, in such case? It was given in view of transgressions and promulgated by angels, at the hands of a mediator; it was to be valid only until that

> descendant or offspring came to whom the promise had been given. Now there can be no mediator when only one person is involved; and God is one.

*NIV:*

> What, then, was the purpose of the law? It was added because of transgressions until the Seed to whom the promise referred had come. The law was put into effect through angels by a mediator. A mediator, however, does not represent just one party; but God is one.

There is clearly more divergence among the translations of Gal 3:19-20 than there was in the case of Mk 1:14-15. Is any of this due to reliance upon different Greek texts? No. The only ancient variant reading occurs at the beginning of the passage in the Greek word *parabaseōn* translated as "transgressions" in my version, RSV, NAB, and NIV and by similar terms in the other texts. Instead of *parabaseōn* ("transgressions") several manuscripts contain the word *praxeōn* ("acts") and one Greek witness reads *paradoseōn* ("traditions"). The translators in all six English versions have rejected the readings "acts" and "traditions" presumably because they are poorly attested in the manuscript tradition and because they do not fit the flow of Paul's argument in Galatians 3. Therefore what differences exist among the six translations cannot be attributed to dependence on a different textual base.

The differences arise from the inherent difficulty of the text to be translated. According to Paul the Law was something "additional" to the promise given to Abraham, and all the translations bring that out. But the effect of this addition poses a problem of interpretation. Why was the Law added? It has something to do with "transgressions" or "crimes." But what precisely? The RSV, NAB, and NIV translate the Greek literally and refuse to hazard a guess about Paul's meaning in their translations. The other three versions are bolder: "to make wrongdoing a legal offence" (NEB), "in order to show what wrongdoing is" (GNB/TEV), and "to specify crimes" (JB). Paul's idea that the purpose of the Law was to show people more clearly than previously what sin is seems to be operative in this passage (see also Rom 4:15; 5:13-14; 5:20; 7:7-13 for the same concept), and the NEB, GNB/TEV, and JB try to bring it out.

Another problem of translation is involved in the word "seed" (*sperma*). In Gal 3:16 Paul insisted that the promise was made to Abraham and to his "seed" (see Gen 12:7; 13:15; 15:18; 17:7-8; 22:16-18; 24:7). The fact that "seed" is singular (actually a collective noun) and not a plural meant in Paul's system of biblical interpretation that the OT texts recounting God's promises to Abraham were really talking about Jesus Christ. The seed is Christ! The Law was provisional until Christ the true seed of Abraham should come. The six translations handle "seed" in Gal 3:19 in a variety of ways ranging from the cautious "the offspring" (RSV) to the explicit "Abraham's descendant" (GNB/TEV). The NIV's "the Seed" has the advantage of being literal while leaving no doubt by its capitalization that the reference is to Jesus Christ.

Other difficult phrases in the passage (the promise, the promulgation of the Law) may deserve consideration, but the phrase about the need for an intermediary seems to be the most awkward in the text. My literal translation indicates that the Greek is very rough: "now the intermediary is not of one." Nevertheless, Paul's point seems clear enough. He contrasts the promise made by God directly to Abraham with the Law given by angels, presumably through an angelic mediator (see Jubilees 1—2; Acts 7:37-38,53), to Israel through Moses. Note that the GNB/TEV wrongly identifies the mediator as "a man" (Moses?). The giving of the Law demanded mediators (see Lev 26:46 and Deut 5:5), while the promise to Abraham did not. A transaction between two groups (angels and Israel) demands two go-betweens, but a transaction between individuals (God and Abraham) does not. According to Paul's logic the presence of mediators proves the inferiority of the Law. The translations all try to bring out the force of the logical principle invoked at the beginning of v.20: One person (here, God) does not need a mediator.

Because the precise meaning of this passage is so problematic, Gal 3:19-20 demonstrates concretely the varying philosophies of translation operative in the six versions. The RSV most closely mirrors the ambiguities of the Greek text, and the GNB/TEV makes the most obvious effort to state what Paul seemed to have meant to say. Between these two ends of the spectrum the NIV here stands nearest to the RSV on the side of literalness, while the NEB and (to a lesser extent) the JB tend toward dynamic equivalence. The NAB appears to strike a balance between formal correspondence and dynamic equivalence.

### C. *Using the Translations Effectively*

All these translations are based on the kind of Greek text of the New Testament judged by the criteria of modern specialists in textual criticism to be superior to the "Received Text," represented in the King James Version, and to the Latin Vulgate underlying the Douay Version. The translators have typically used a modern edition such as the Nestle-Aland *Novum Testamentum Graece* or the United Bible Societies' *Greek New Testament* without taking on themselves the obligation of rigidly adhering to that text alone. As we already saw, textual criticism involves the interpretation of the text, and frequently the process of translation can reveal the superiority on internal grounds of one reading over another. These modern translators reserve the right to depart occasionally from the printed Greek text when they are convinced that the printed text can be improved. The most important departures or variants are usually noted at the foot of the page by expressions like "other ancient authorities read . . ." or "some early manuscripts add . . . ."

In addition to the problems encountered in rendering problematic words or phrases in specific passages, translators of the Bible face certain general problems that make their task considerably more difficult than it may appear at first glance. The documents contained in the New Testament arose from a culture that is very different from that of the twentieth century, and it is always hard to know the extent to which one has to go to make those documents intelligible for people today. A rigidly literal translation is finally no translation at all. But neither is a paraphrase. Furthermore, to whom are these documents being made intelligible? Both manual laborers and college professors have the right to understand the Bible. But will one and the same translation be suitable for both groups? This raises the related issue of the multiple purposes for which these translations are designed and used. For example, several of the versions (RSV, NAB, JB) are used not only for private study but also in public worship. But is it proper to cut up an existing Bible translation into liturgical segments without looking also to its effectiveness in oral communication? Finally the English language itself changes. The use of "man" as a generic term for "human being" seemed to be perfectly acceptable English fifteen years ago but is now condemned as "sexist." The revision committees of the six English translations discussed in this chapter will eventually have to confront the serious problem of sexist language in the Bible. The two-thousand year cultural gap, the literary level at which to pitch the translation, the multiple and sometimes conflicting purposes for which the translations are used, and sexist language—these are only a few of the general problems facing translators of the Bible into modern English.

The terms "dynamic equivalence" and "formal correspondence" have appeared several times with reference to the philosophies of translation presupposed in the six modern English versions discussed here. Even the least literal versions make the explicit claim to be translations rather than paraphrases, but it may not be clear to all how this claim can be valid. The reason is the translation philosophy of dynamic equivalence. A dynamic equivalence type of translation (NEB, GNB/TEV, JB) tries to transform the information that the ancient authors meant to convey to their original readers in such a way that modern readers will react to this information in the same way that the authors meant their readers to react. Rather than producing a word-by-word rendition that is bound to the sentence structures and patterns of expression of the original text, the translator who relies on the philosophy of dynamic equivalence steps back from the text, investigates the meanings of its words and structures, and transfers the message of the text into the so-called "receptor language." Dynamic equivalence involves looking at units of communication and not at individual words or phrases in isolation. Dynamic equivalence involves transferring and restructuring the parts of the original message into the structures and speech patterns of the receptor language.

The obvious danger in dynamic equivalence translations is the possibility that the message of the original text may be misunderstood. The resulting translation then would have no genuine foundation in the text, and the readers of the translation would have no chance of reconstructing the original text for themselves. A formal correspondence translation like the RSV presents the biblical text in intelligible English but takes far less initiative in determining for the reader what the text meant for its original readers and what it means for today. The dynamic equivalence translations have the advantage of reflecting more explicitly the opinions of experts regarding the interpretation of the text then and now. The formal correspondence translations leave the readers with a better possibility of exploring for themselves the various options involved in the text and of coming to their own decisions about its present-day relevance.

This discussion of modern English translations began with two questions: Why are there so many new translations of the Bible? Which one is the best? The answer to the first question should be clear by now, but the second question still needs a response. Which modern English translation is the best? The answer is that it depends on what you are looking for. If you want a reliable "formal correspondence" translation, choose the RSV (or the NAB or the NIV). If you want an intelligent and intelligible "dynamic equivalence" translation, choose the NEB or GNB/TEV or the JB. If you want more information about the texts, look at the valuable introductions and notes in the JB or NAB or in one of the annotated editions of the RSV or NEB. The days of relying on a single English translation are over. Now it is a matter of using the existing translations in an intelligent and creative way. If one is serious about understanding a particular text, then it is often useful to use one formal correspondence translation along with one or more dynamic equivalence translations. Where there is a significant difference among the translations, the interpreter should ask how the difference arose and consult the notes accompanying the translation or a reliable commentary to find out why. In this way the comparison of various translations can serve as an occasion for increased understanding of and sensitivity to the meaning of the text. Instead of looking upon the many English translations of the Bible as rivals or competitors, we might turn the situation to our own advantage and use them as complements to one another in the task of understanding the biblical text.

## *Bibliography: Translations*

*Modern English Translations*

*Good News Bible with Deuterocanonicals/Apocrypha. The Bible in Today's English Version* (New York: American Bible Society. 1979).

*The Holy Bible. New International Version. Containing the Old Testament and The New Testament* (Grand Rapids: Zondervan, 1978).

*The Holy Bible Containing the Old and New Testaments. Revised Standard Version* (New York: United Bible Societies, 1971).

*The Jerusalem Bible* (Garden City, NY: Doubleday, 1966; revised, 1985).

*The New American Bible. Translated from the Original Languages with Critical Use of All the Ancient Sources* (Paterson, N.J.: St. Anthony Guild, 1970; revised, 1987).

*The New English Bible with the Apocrypha* (New York: Oxford University Press and Cambridge University Press, 1970).

*Guides to English Translations*

L.R. Bailey (ed.), *The Word of God. A Guide to English Versions of the Bible* (Atlanta: John Knox, 1982).

J. Beekman and J. Callow, *Translating the Word of God* (Grand Rapids: Zondervan, 1974).

F.F. Bruce, *History of the Bible in English. From the earliest versions* (3rd ed. New York: Oxford University Press, 1978).

S. Kubo and W.F. Specht, *So Many Versions? Twentieth-Century English Versions of the Bible* (rev. ed.; Grand Rapids: Zondervan, 1983).

J.P. Lewis, *The English Bible from KJV to NIV. A History and Evaluation* (Grand Rapids: Baker, 1981).

J.L. Mays (ed.), *Interpretation* 32 (1978) 115-70.

D. McCall (ed.), *Review and Expositor* 76 (1979) 297-416.

E.A. Nida and C.R. Taber. *The Theory and Practice of Translation.* Leiden: Brill, 1969.

# 4. WORDS AND MOTIFS

## *A. The Language of the New Testament*

WE HAVE SEEN how textual critics attempt to establish the original form of the Greek text of the New Testament, and we have also seen something about the character of and philosophy behind six widely circulated English translations. This chapter is concerned with the ways by which we get from a Greek text first written some nineteen hundred years ago to our reliable modern versions. It is concerned with the meanings of the words and the motifs used in the New Testament writings. As we have seen, translating the New Testament is not simply a matter of consulting a list of Greek-English equivalences and mechanically substituting one for the other. This is precisely why efforts at translation by computers fare so poorly. The transfer of thoughts and feelings from one culture to another, especially when this involves moving from one language to another, is a very complicated process. Every effort must be made to capture the nuances of the words and motifs used in the New Testament if the translation is to have any claim to accuracy.

One of the very common tasks in biblical scholarship today is to study the use of a word or a theme in a particular book or in the New Testament as a whole or in the entire Bible. Done in a rigidly philological way with a primary interest in etymology and range of meanings, it is an exercise in lexicography. Done in a linguistic-philosophical way where the interest is in the deep structures of the mind and in the possible modes of communication, it shares in the contemporary developments in the theory of language. Done in a meditative key with a concern for the religious values communicated by the words, it is a method of doing biblical theology. Clearly the study of words and motifs in the New Testament has a pivotal position not only in the process of translation but also in the whole task of biblical interpretation.

The New Testament is a Greek book. Though there may well be Hebrew or Aramaic traditions in the background of some passages and though there are a few loanwords in it from other ancient languages (Latin, Aramaic, Hebrew), the New Testament consists of twenty-seven documents that were composed in Greek. Yet anyone who has studied the classical Greek of Plato or Demosthenes is in for a surprise on picking up the New Testament. The Greek of the New Testament is quite a bit different from that used in Athens in the fifth and fourth centuries B.C. Even in the third century A.D. opponents of Christianity like Celsus noticed this and took it as proof of Christianity's "inferior" character. Apologists for Christianity replied that the apostles were simply adapting their speech to the simple people in their audiences or that the apostles themselves were simple people. Others thought that the content of Christianity had brought about a linguistic revolution of some sort and that the New Testament represents a kind of "Holy Ghost Greek." This view of New Testament Greek as unique, which has learned defenders even today, assumes that despite differences among them the New Testament books represent one linguistic world and that this linguistic world was to some degree sealed off from the rest of the Greek-speaking world. Still others attributed the peculiar character of New Testament Greek to the fact that the native language of the biblical writers was Hebrew or Aramaic and that the patterns of thought and expression from these languages had influenced the kind of Greek appearing in the New Testament.

All three of these explanations have a grain of truth. The New Testament writings were intended for a wider audience than most of the Greek or Latin classics. The content of Christian faith does exercise some influence on the language in which it is expressed. There are Semitic influences on New Testament Greek. But the discovery of Greek papyrus documents in Egypt toward the end of the nineteenth century showed that the New Testament represents the late Greek colloquial language known even in antiquity as the "Koine" or "the common" language. Up to this point the debate about the character of New Testament Greek had taken as the point of comparison the classical literary documents and their later imitations. But the Greek papyri from Egypt came from roughly around the time of Jesus and the rise of the early church and included business documents, deeds, marriage contracts, IOU's, and so forth. These documents are written in approximately the same kind of Greek as the New Testament and proved that by and large the New Testament is the product of ordinary life in the period and speaks the Greek that ordinary people spoke and wrote. That ordinary language is Koine Greek—a language formed from the old dialects (Ionic, Attic, Doric, Aeolic) in a mixture to which the Attic dialect made the greatest contribution. It reached a homogeneous form by the time of Alexander the Great and spread throughout the Hellenistic world. Besides the New Testament and the Greek papyri from Egypt, there are other sources for Koine Greek: nonliterary sources (other papyri, inscriptions, ostraca), non-Christian authors (Polybius, Plutarch, Diodorus, etc), Hellenistic-Jewish sources (Septuagint, Philo, Josephus, etc.), ancient Christian writings, and some facets of medieval and modern Greek. So the Greek of the New Testament turns out to be not so peculiar after all.

How does one go about studying a term or a motif in the New Testament? A good start is to consult a concordance, a lexicon, and a theological dictionary. Bibliographic information and descriptions of the many such reliable tools available to the biblical student can be found in J.A.

Fitzmyer, *Introductory Bibliography for the Study of Scripture* (Subsidia Biblica 3; rev. ed.; Rome: Biblical Institute Press, 1981). Here we need describe only one example of each genre as a means of initiating the reader into the usefulness and limitations of these reference works.

A *concordance* is an alphabetical index of the principal words of a book with the references to the passages in which each word occurs and usually some part of the context. Indispensable in New Testament research is W. F. Moulton and A. S. Geden, *A Concordance to the Greek Testament According to the Texts of Westcott and Hort, Tischendorf and the English Revisers* (5th rev. ed. by H. K. Moulton; Edinburgh: T. & T. Clark, 1978). First published in 1897, this concordance is based not on the Byzantine textual tradition of the so-called Textus Receptus but on the superior form of textual tradition represented in the modern editions of the Greek New Testament over the past one hundred years. Though "and" (*kai*) and the particle *de* are omitted, this concordance is comprehensive to the point that Geden in the preface (p. v) claims that the principles of inclusion preclude "the omission of any expression which, by even a remote probability, might be regarded as forming part of the true text of the New Testament."

The concordance cites the Greek word (for example, *baptizō* meaning "I baptize") and then lists each occurrence of this word according to book, chapter, and verse (e.g. Mt 3:6) in keeping with the usual order of New Testament books (Mt, Mk, Lk, Jn, Acts, Rom, etc.). Beside each reference the concordance supplies the keyword in its context in Greek: "and they were baptized by him in the river Jordan." There is also a code (1, 2, 3, 4, 5) indicating the major classes of occurrences; for example, with the preposition "in" or "into" or with the nouns in the dative case. So the concordance allows the user to see at a glance all the occurrences of specific terms in their contexts. Most of the English translations discussed in the previous chapter now have concordances. For instance, see J. W. Ellison, *Nelson's Complete Concordance of the Revised Standard*

*Version Bible* (New York: Thomas Nelson, 1957). An example of a thematic or topical concordance keyed to the English Jerusalem Bible but usable with other versions is M. Darton (ed.), *Modern Concordance to the New Testament* (Garden City, NY: Doubleday, 1976).

*Lexicon* is a term applied to dictionaries or wordbooks of ancient languages like Hebrew, Greek, and Latin. Practically speaking, it allows one to distinguish such inventories from the theological and historical encyclopedias that carry the title of "dictionary" in the New Testament field. The most important lexicon is *A Greek-English Lexicon of the New Testament and Other Early Christian Literature* (Chicago: University of Chicago Press, 1979) compiled in German by W. Bauer, translated into English and edited by W. F. Arndt and F. W. Gingrich, and newly revised by F. W. Danker. A typical article in the lexicon cites the Greek word (e.g. *baptizō*) in its various verbal forms and supplies the basic meaning ("dip, immerse"). Then it organizes the various uses of the term according to categories: (1) of Jewish ritual washings; (2) in the special sense of baptize—of John the Baptist, of Christian baptism (performed by Jesus' disciples, baptize in or with respect to the name of someone, with the purpose given); (3) in the figurative sense, though related to the idea of Christian baptism—typologically of Israel's passage through the Red Sea, in the Holy Spirit, of martyrdom. At each point the article supplies the references to New Testament texts and to relevant extrabiblical parallels along with information about modern scholarly contributions. The lexicon supplies the user with a sense for the range of meanings that a given word can carry and for the various categories into which the individual usages fall. Of course, Bauer's lexicon should be used alongside a resource like *A Greek Grammar of the New Testament and Other Early Christian Literature* (Chicago: University of Chicago Press, 1961), which is R. W. Funk's translation and edition of a grammar compiled in German by F. Blass and revised by A. Debrunner.

One of the great achievements of German New Testament scholarship in the twentieth century is now available in

English as *Theological Dictionary of the New Testament*, volumes I-X (Grand Rapids, MI: Eerdmans, 1964-76), which was edited by G. Kittel and G. Friedrich and translated into English by G. W. Bromiley. What Kittel conceived in 1928 as a two-volume project to be carried out by fifteen scholars in three years was completed after forty-five years (1973) and the collaboration of one-hundred-and-five authors in nine volumes (with the index in volume X). It takes up where the concordance and the lexicon leave off. On the other hand, it is not intended as a full-scale commentary on specific passages or as a synthesis of biblical theology. It presents articles on various New Testament words and themes and pays special attention to the meanings of the words in classical and Koine Greek, in the Septuagint and in the Hebrew text underlying it, and in the New Testament. For example, the term *baptō, baptizō* has these six headings: the meaning of *baptō* and *baptizō*, religious washings in Hellenism, *ṭbl* and *baptizein* in the Old Testament and Judaism, the baptism of John, Christian baptism, and baptism as a syncretistic mystery. The quality of scholarship in these articles is very high, and the usefulness of this fundamental tool cannot be overemphasized. A distinguished American scholar (F. W. Danker) has described it as "a fountain where Hebraists slake their philological thirst, classicists drink etymological nectar, and New Testament students find rare theological refreshment."

Not all scholars, however, are as enthusiastic about the *Theological Dictionary* as Danker is. In fact, James Barr in *The Semantics of Biblical Language* (London—New York: Oxford University Press, 1962) made some severe criticisms against the project. Barr's critique does not destroy the validity of the dictionary, but some of his points deserve serious reflection from anyone who wishes to deal with the words and motifs of the New Testament. First, the articles tend to mix up philology and theology by overemphasizing the new meanings given to words by Christian faith. Second, the significance of etymology is sometimes overstressed. Etymology is not a safe guide to meaning unless it is constantly checked by reference to actual usage.

Third, grave dangers result if we insist on attaching theological significance to words taken in isolation, for theological thinking is done primarily in the phrase and the sentence, not in the word. Finally, articles on individual words like *agapaō* ("love") or *hamartia* ("sin") tend to become essays on the biblical notions of love or sin, and then the whole complex is read into every single passage in which the term occurs. These criticisms provide helpful advice about what is to be avoided in dealing with New Testament words and motifs and illustrate the philosophical complexities involved in analyzing and indeed using words as means of human communication.

Concordances, lexicons, and theological dictionaries provide treasures of information and are fascinating in their own right. But how can they contribute to our understanding and appreciation of particular passages in the New Testament? They tell us where else the particular word or motif in the passage under consideration appears and what it means there. The uses of the term in the Septuagint, pagan writings, intertestamental Jewish literature, and in the other books of the New Testament can alert us to its possible meanings in the New Testament text being studied. This kind of inventory of parallel uses is the first step in the process of illumining the meaning of a term in a particular passage. The second step focuses on the singularity of the text itself: What meaning does the term have in this context? This step involves analysis of the brief thought unit in which the term appears as well as the same author's uses of the term elsewhere in his work and the author's general philosophical and theological outlook. The final step demands a return to the reference tools: Where does this instance stand in the term's history? At stake here is not only the history of the term prior to the use in the particular text but also the ways in which the text has been understood at various points in history, and the aim behind such an investigation is to let this use of the term emerge in all its particularity.

By way of summary then, there are three fundamental questions to be asked in studying a term or a motif in the New Testament: Where else does the word appear, and what does it mean there? What meaning does it have in this context (passage, whole document, author's general outlook)? Where does this instance stand in the term's history? The two examples discussed here—the meaning of *ethnē* ("Gentiles") in Mt 28:19 and *doxa* ("glory") in Rom 3:23—illustrate the light that asking such questions can shed on two very important New Testament texts.

## *B. Examples of Word Studies*

1. *Matthew 28:19:* Even a casual reader of Matthew's Gospel senses how important the last scene on the mountain in Galilee is for understanding the Evangelist's aims. Speaking to the eleven disciples, Jesus proclaims that all authority has been given to him and that the eleven are to make disciples of all nations:

> [16]Now the eleven disciples went to Galilee, to the mountain to which Jesus had directed them. [17]And when they saw him they worshiped him; but some doubted. [18]And Jesus came and said to them, "All authority in heaven and on earth has been given to me. [19]Go therefore and make disciples of all nations, baptizing them in the name of the Father and of the Son and of the Holy Spirit, [20]teaching them to observe all that I have commanded you; and lo, I am with you always, to the close of the age."

Many questions emerge from this text, but what concerns us here is the extent of "all nations." Does "all nations" include Israel, or does it refer to all but Israel? It is important to be precise about the literary-historical level at which the question is being asked. Our interest here is in what the Evangelist whom we call "Matthew" meant when he placed this passage at the conclusion of his Gospel. At this point we are not concerned with what the risen Lord or the transmitters of the pre-Matthean tradition or interpreters throughout the ages may have meant by it. The question then is this: Did the person who put the Gospel of Matthew into final form mean "all the nations" (including Israel) or "all the Gentiles" when he cited the risen Lord's command to preach the gospel?

The obvious first step in answering the question is to determine what the problematic term is. The Greek word is *ethnē*, the plural of the Greek neuter noun *ethnos* meaning "nation." The Greek root has made its way into English as "ethnic." A glance at the concordance to the Greek translation of the Old Testament shows that *ethnē* is the usual way of rendering the Hebrew *gôyîm*. In the early stages of the Hebrew Bible *gôyîm* refers to the nations in competition with Israel (Edom, Egypt, Assyria, etc.) but in post-exilic times it tends to describe the collectivity of nations other than Israel and the individual representatives of those nations. In a few passages of the Septuagint it refers to "non-Jewish humanity," and in several places in the New Testament *ethnē* clearly means "Gentiles" (see Rom 11:11-13 and Gal 2:12) as opposed to "Jews." So at the time when Matthew's Gospel was written the Greek word *ethnē* that appears in the problematic phrase in Mt 28:19 could be used to refer to that collective of non-Jews that we call "the Gentiles."

What does *ethnos/ethnē* mean elsewhere in Matthew's Gospel? If it can be shown that the term always or almost always has the clear meaning of "Gentiles" in Matthew's Gospel, then it is highly probable that it carries this same meaning in Mt 28:19. The word appears in three passages in which the three Synoptic Gospels have a common text: Mt 20:19 (Mk 10:33; Lk 18:33); Mt 20:25 (Mk 10:42; Lk 22:25); and Mt 24:7 (Mk 13:8; Lk 21:10). In the first two cases ("and deliver him to the *ethnē* to be mocked and scourged and crucified" and "the rulers of the *ethnē* lord it over them") the meaning is clearly "Gentiles," while the third text ("*ethnos* will rise against *ethnos*") is moot. In the two other instances of shared tradition ("the *ethnē* seek all these things" [Mt 6:32; Lk 12:30]) and "you will be hated by all the *ethnē* for my sake" [Mt 24:9; Mk 13:13; Lk 21:17]) the meaning "the Gentiles" is likely. The term *ethnos* / *ethnē* occurs nine times in material that is peculiar to Matthew (4:15; 10:5,18; 12:18,21; 21:43; 24:14; 25:32; 28:19), and in nearly every case the clear meaning is "the Gentiles"; that is, not including Israel. For example, in Mt 10:18 ("and you will be dragged before governors and kings for my sake, to bear testimony before them and the *ethnē*") the sufferings of the disciples, inflicted by both Jews and Gentiles, will serve as a witness to the Gentiles. The saying in Mt 21:43 ("the kingdom of God will be taken away from you and given to an *ethnos* producing the fruits of it") comes at the end of the parable of the wicked husbandmen and contrasts Israel and the new collective, the church, which is composed indiscriminately of Jews and Gentiles who receive the preaching of the kingdom and act upon it. So at every level in the Gospel the usual meaning of *ethnos* and *ethnē* does not seem to include Israel.

Does the insertion of the adjective "all" before *ethnē* change the meaning of the word? Granted that *ethnē* usually means "Gentiles" in Matthew, does that meaning change when the phrase becomes "all the nations?" The expression occurs in Mt 24:9,14; 25:32; and 28:19, but the most important of these is 25:32: "Before him will be gathered all the *ethnē*, and he will separate them." The sentence occurs at the beginning of the parable of the sheep and the goats—the vision of the last judgment found in Mt 25:31-46. Does the judgment in Mt 25:32 refer to all nations including Israel, or could it be a judgment only for the Gentiles as opposed to the Jews? Surprisingly enough there are many Jewish texts from Jesus' time that seem to envision separate judgments for Jews and Gentiles (see 2 Baruch 72; Psalms of Solomon 17:27-28; 4 Ezra 13:33-49; 1 Enoch 90:20-27; 91:12-15; Testament of Benjamin 10:8-9). There are even hints in some New Testament texts that the last judgment involves different groups in different ways. In 1 Pt 4:17 judgment is said to begin with the household of God and end with the godless. The statement in 1 Cor 6:2-3 that the saints are to judge the world and the angels presupposes a prior judgment for Christians (see also Mt 19:28). Rom 2:9-10 provides the clearest indication of separate judgments for Jews and Gentiles: "There will be tribulation and distress for every human being who does evil, the Jew first and also the Greek, but glory and honor and peace for every one who does good, the Jew first and also the Greek." The point is that the instance of "all the *ethnē*" in the context of the last judgment in Mt 25:32 does not prove that the phrase must include Israel.

Is the interpretation of all the *ethnē* as Gentiles in Mt 28:19 consistent with Matthew's historical situation and theological outlook? The Gospel reflects a definite split between the churches and the synagogues. Even Christians of Jewish origin no longer belong to "their synagogues" (4:23; 9:35; 10:17; 12:9; 13:54), which are viewed as the synagogues of the hypocrites (6:2,5; 23:6,34). In a predominantly Jewish-Christian community like Matthew's the time of the mission to Israel seems to be over. Israel *qua* Israel has ceased to play a significant role in salvation history as Matthew read it (see 21:41,43), and now it is the time to spend energy upon preaching the gospel to the Gentiles. Within this historical and theological setting the risen Lord's command to make disciples of all the Gentiles could galvanize the community into action.

A final line of evidence is provided by some early Christian commentators on this and related Matthean texts. When discussing Mt 13:57 Origen says: "Since a prophet has no honor in his own country, when the Jews did not receive the Word, they [the disciples] went away to the *ethnē*." Eusebius says: "And he bids his own disciples after their rejection: 'Go and make disciples of all the *ethnē* in my name.' So, then, we that are *ethnē* know and receive the prophet that was foretold . . . while the Jewish nation (*ethnos*), not receiving him that was foretold, has paid the fit penalty." John Chrysostom in his homily on Jn 17:1-5 states: "For then he [Jesus] said: 'Go not into the road of the *ethnē*.' But afterwards he would say: 'Go, make disciples of all the *ethnē*' and declare that the Father also wills this. This scandalized the Jews very much and even the disciples." Such quotations indicate that intelligent Greek-speaking Christians of the third and fourth centuries A.D. understood Mt 28:19 as referring to making disciples of the Gentiles.

So all five lines of evidence—the meaning of *ethnē* in Jewish and Christian texts other than the Gospel, its usual meaning in Matthew, the absence of a special meaning for "all the *ethnē*," the history and theology of the Matthean community, and the opinions of some Greek-speaking Fathers of the church—indicate that Matthew meant "make disciples of all the Gentiles" in 28:19. A more detailed presentation of this argument can be found in the article "'Make Disciples of All the Gentiles' (Matthew 28:19)" by D. R. A. Hare and D. J. Harrington, which was published in *Catholic Biblical Quarterly* 37 (1975) 359-369. Readers of that article should also consult J. P. Meier's article "Nations or Gentiles in Matthew 28:19?" in *Catholic Biblical Quarterly* 39 (1977) 94-102 for an opposing viewpoint.

2. *Romans 3:23:* In his letter to the Romans, Paul begins his presentation of Christian faith by showing that both Gentiles (1:18-32) and Jews (2:1—3:20) were under the power of sin. Before putting forth Abraham as the model of faithful response to God (4:1-25), he summarizes his case in 3:23-24: "since all have sinned and fall short of the glory of God, they are justified by his grace as a gift . . . ." Someone whose sole contact with Greek was the study of classical authors might be surprised at the translation of the expression *tēs doxēs tou theou* in Rom 3:23 as "the glory of God." The word *doxa* in Greek usually means something like "expectation," "opinion," or "estimation." How did it come to be translated as "glory?"

The pre-Christian Greek translation of the Hebrew Old Testament, which is called the Septuagint, supplies the answer. There *doxa* is the usual translation of the Hebrew term *kābôd,* whose basic meaning is "weighty." The *kābôd* of God is the something "weighty" which gives him importance, which makes him impressive, the force of his self-manifestation. In the Septuagint the *doxa tou theou* is the "divine glory" which reveals the nature of God in creation and in his acts—that which fills heaven and earth. So the use of *doxa* as the Greek equivalent of *kābôd* ("glory") represents a decisive shift in the history of that term. Gerhard Kittel in his article on *doxa* in the *Theological Dictionary* described the achievement of the Septuagint translator(s) in this way: "Taking a word for opinion which implies all the subjectivity and all the vacillation of human views and conjectures, he made it express something absolutely objective, i.e. the reality of God."

In Rom 3:23 Paul used *doxa tou theou* according to the pattern of the Septuagint to say that sinners—Gentiles and Jews alike—display little of the divine nature according to which and for which they were created (see Rom 8:17-18, 21). Left to their own devices, all fall short of the glory of God. Without the free gift of God, right relationship with God or justification would be impossible. This example illustrates one of the very important influences on the kind of Greek found in the New Testament—the Greek usage found in the Septuagint, which was the Bible of the Greek-speaking Christian communities.

## *Bibliography: Words and Motifs*


P.J. Achtemeier (ed.), *Harper's Bible Dictionary* (San Francisco: Harper & Row, 1985).

J. Barr, *The Semantics of Biblical Language* (New York: Oxford University Press, 1961).

J.B. Bauer (ed.), *Encyclopedia of Biblical Theology. The Complete Sacramentum Verbi* (New York: Crossroad, 1981).

W. Bauer, *A Greek-English Lexicon of the New Testament and Other Early Christian Literature* (tr. and ed. W.F. Arndt and F.W. Gingrich, rev. F.W. Danker; Chicago: University of Chicago Press, 1979).

G.W. Bromiley (ed.), *Theological Dictionary of the New Testament Abridged in One Volume* (Grand Rapids: Eerdmans, 1985).

G.B. Caird, *The Language and Imagery of the Bible* (Philadelphia: Westminster, 1980).

G. Kittel and G. Friedrich (eds.), *Theological Dictionary of the New Testament,* vols. I-X (Grand Rapids: Eerdmans, 1964-76).

J.P. Louw, *Semantics of New Testament Greek* (Philadelphia: Fortress, 1982).

C. Morrison, *An Analytical Concordance to the Revised Standard Version of The New Testament* (Philadelphia: Westminster, 1979).

W.F. Moulton and A.S. Geden, *A Concordance to the Greek Testament According to the Texts of Westcott and Hort, Tischendorf and the English Revisers* (5th rev. ed. by H.K. Moulton; Edinburgh: T. & T. Clark, 1978).

N. Turner, *Christian Words* (Edinburgh: Clark, 1980).

M. Zerwick and M. Grosvenor, *A Grammatical Analysis of the Greek New Testament* (2 vols.; Rome: Biblical Institute Press, 1974, 1979).

# 5. SOURCE CRITICISM

## *A. Detecting Sources in New Testament Documents*

THE CITATION of an already existing source is a natural part of everyday communication. How often do we say, "he said this" or "I read that in the newspaper!" In school we were instructed to be very careful about making clear when we were relying upon sources. We were duly warned about the need for using quotation marks and giving full bibliographic information in the footnotes. Even when we borrowed someone else's idea and put it in our own words, we were told to specify our sources. People in antiquity were not as careful as we moderns usually are in indicating our sources. They might say "as X writes," but they did not use quotation marks or footnotes. Part of this apparent carelessness is explained by the fact that in ancient times originality of authorship was not the sacred matter that it is to us today. Apart from the classical authors like Horace or Vergil who wrote with financial support from wealthy patrons, authors in antiquity often published their works anonymously or even put them forth pseudonymously under the name of their teachers or of famous figures from the past.

Although the old and natural issue of trying to isolate the sources of a literary composition is a good deal more complicated in an ancient work like the New Testament than it is in a modern work, the questions to be asked remain much the same: (1) Did the document being studied have a source before it? (2) What did that source say?

(3) What was the relationship of the author to the source (exact copy? misunderstanding? change?)? Determining the source's presence, the source's meaning, and how the source was used—these are the three obvious concerns of source criticism. Attention to these issues can aid us in understanding the history of the movement that produced the text and in understanding the author's own intentions and achievements.

Source criticism is a fairly simple operation when the author tells us that he is using a source. For example, Matthew in 1:23 cites a passage from Isaiah 7:14: "Behold, a virgin shall conceive and bear a son, and his name shall be called Emmanuel." In the preceding verse (1:22) he made it clear that he relied upon a source: "All this took place to fulfill what the Lord had spoken by the prophet." In such an instance, source criticism is a matter of determining precisely what the source was (Is 7:14), what that passage meant in the original Hebrew context of the book of Isaiah and what changes in meaning may have occurred in the process of translation into Greek, and how the Evangelist used the passage in explaining the origin and identity of Jesus.

Luke, however, is the only New Testament writer who makes an explicit claim to have had access to nonbiblical sources on a large scale. In the prologue to his two-volume story of early Christianity (Luke-Acts) he speaks of the "many" people who "have undertaken to compile a narrative of the things which have been accomplished among us." Presumably Luke knew these writings at first hand and made use of them in his own composition. Unfortunately he does not tell us where he relies on sources and where he composes on his own, and so modern scholars have had to exercise their considerable ingenuity on trying to isolate Luke's sources. For example, it has been argued that the first half of Acts is a translation from an Aramaic original and is markedly different in literary style from the remainder of the book. But others have explained the same data as due to the influence of the Greek of the Septuagint upon

Luke's literary style. In the second half of Acts there are several passages (16:10-17; 20:5-15; 21:1-18; 27:1—28:16) in which the first-personal plural pronoun "we" is prominent. The author of these "we"-passages seems to have been a participant in Paul's travels. These passages have been variously interpreted as a coherent source that Luke had obtained, as excerpts from Luke's own travel journal as he accompanied Paul, or as an example of an ancient literary device used only to add vividness to the narrative. The existence of a pre-Lukan "we" source still remains a matter of debate.

How does one detect the presence of sources in the New Testament documents? A look at Paul's letters may make us aware of some useful criteria for isolating sources. The most obvious criterion is Paul's own statement that he is citing this or that Old Testament passage. A variety of formulas are used; for example, "as it is written" (Rom 1:17), "as indeed he says in Hosea" (Rom 9:25), and "and as Isaiah predicted" (Rom 9:29). In other instances a close analysis of the text of 1 Corinthians suggests that Paul replied to a written (or oral) report of happenings in Corinth: "Now concerning the matters about which you wrote (1 Cor 7:1a)." The sentence that follows ("It is well for a man not to touch a woman") may have been a slogan popular among the ascetic members of the Corinthian church. Then there is a series of replies to the questions asked in the source: "now concerning the unmarried" (1 Cor 7:25); "now concerning food offered to idols" (8:1); "now concerning spiritual gifts" (12:1); "now concerning the contribution for the saints" (16:1); and "as for our brother Apollos" (16:12). Furthermore, there are points at which Paul repeats the slogans of his opponents: "I belong to Apollos" (1 Cor 1:12); "all things are lawful for me" (1 Cor 6:12); "food is meant for the stomach and the stomach for food" (1 Cor 6:13). Even though there are no quotation marks in the Greek text, it is clear to the discerning reader that Paul is citing Scripture or replying to a letter or answering his opponents in these instances. In writing to the early Christian communities Paul clearly made use of sources.

The presence of sources can also be determined on internal grounds. For example, when a passage interrupts the flow of thought and/or uses a different kind of language from the surrounding context, one can legitimately suspect the use of a source even though no explicit indication has been given. In 2 Cor 6:1-13 Paul makes a plea for his reconciliation with the Corinthian community and urges them to widen their hearts as he has widened his own heart (see vv.11-13). The plea for openness of heart and reconciliation is resumed in 2 Cor 7:2-4, but in the midst of this plea is a passage about avoiding relations with unbelievers (6:14—7:1). The fact that 2 Cor 6:14—7:1 interrupts the flow of thought is an initial argument in favor of taking it as an independent literary source. This suspicion is confirmed by the presence of several words not found elsewhere in Paul's writings ("mismated," "partnership," "accord," "in common," "Beliar," "defilement"). There is some debate as to whether Paul himself cited this source or it has been inserted here by a later editor, but consideration of the passage does reveal two important internal criteria for detecting sources—interruption of the flow of thought and the use of unusual words.

Among the most important kinds of sources that Paul cited are summaries of faith and hymns. The parade example of a pre-Pauline confession of faith appears in 1 Cor 15:3-5:

> [3]For I delivered to you as of first importance what I also received, that Christ died for our sins in accordance with the scriptures, [4]that he was buried, that he was raised on the third day in accordance with the scriptures, [5]and that he appeared to Cephas, then to the twelve.

Here Paul tips us off to his use of a source by his introduction: "For I delivered to you as of first importance what I also received." He puts the summary forth as something that he had received from his predecessors in the Christian faith and had handed on to the people of Corinth.

It is theological common-ground for Paul and the Corinthians as he begins his discussion of the resurrection of the dead.

Detection of the presence of a pre-Pauline hymn in Phil 2:6-11 is not quite so easy, but most New Testament scholars consider it certain that Paul used a well-known hymn about Christ to illustrate his teaching on humility:

> [5]Have this mind among yourselves, which is yours in Christ Jesus, [6]who, though he was in the form of God, did not count equality with God a thing to be grasped, [7]but emptied himself, taking the form of a servant, being born in the likeness of men. [8]And being found in human form he humbled himself and became obedient unto death, even death on a cross. [9]Therefore God has highly exalted him and bestowed on him the name which is above every name, [10]that at the name of Jesus every knee should bow, in heaven and on earth and under the earth, [11]and every tongue confess that Jesus Christ is Lord, to the glory of God the Father.

The presence of rare and not characteristically Pauline expressions establishes Phil 2:6-11 as a pre-Pauline piece: "form," "equality with God," "a thing to be grasped," "emptied," "highly exalted." The use of participles, the use of parallel phrases (similar to the poetic conventions of the Old Testament), and the rhythmic quality of the sentences suggest that the pre-Pauline source was a hymn used in the early church. The people at Philippi probably knew and used this hymn, and its appearance in Paul's letter would have provided them with a Christological basis for encouraging their efforts at humility.

The reading of Paul's letters illustrates the most important ways of detecting the presence of sources within a document. Sometimes the writer will make it clear to us that a source was used by introducing citations of Scripture with stereotyped formulas ("as it is written") or by introducing a traditional confession of faith with an appropriate expression ("for I delivered to you as of first importance what I also received"). At other times the discerning reader will easily recognize that the writer is replying to a previous communication ("now concerning . . .") or is citing a slogan to be refuted ("I am of Apollos"). In all these cases there are external grounds for concluding that sources have been used. Where the author does not come out and tell us, there are some internal grounds for suspecting the presence of a source: a radically different vocabulary and literary style from what is found elsewhere in the document, a violent interruption of the flow of thought, and the introduction of unusual theological emphases in the course of an argument.

A special and most important case of source analysis is presented by the first three Gospels. The Gospels of Matthew, Mark, and Luke have traditionally been called the "Synoptic" Gospels because they share a "common vision" of Jesus. John's Gospel goes its own way and has long been known as "the spiritual Gospel." Learned people throughout the ages like Clement of Alexandria and Augustine, had noticed the close relationships among the first three Gospels, but only in the latter part of the eighteenth century did the matter begin to be investigated methodically. The German New Testament scholar J. J. Griesbach proposed this hypothesis (which is enjoying something of a revival today in some circles): Matthew's Gospel was used by Luke as a source, and Mark used both Matthew and Luke as sources. That means that Matthew was the earliest Gospel and Mark the latest of the three.

As the nineteenth century progressed and passed into the twentieth, however, the Griesbach hypothesis of Synoptic relationships receded in popularity. More and more critical scholars began to view Mark as the first Gospel chronologically. Matthew reproduces ninety percent of Mark, and Luke reproduces fifty percent of it. Most of Mark's words are reproduced by Matthew and/or Luke. Mark's order of events seems to have been adopted by Matthew and Luke. Furthermore, Mark's rough Greek style seems to have been polished by Matthew and Luke independently. Besides countering these positive arguments, there are several matters that opponents of Markan priority need to explain: Why would anyone want to abbreviate or conflate Matthew and Luke to produce a Gospel like Mark? Why was so much of Matthew and Luke omitted by Mark? In particular, why did Mark omit the infancy stories and the post-resurrection accounts? What kind of theologian does Mark turn out to be if he really had access to Matthew and/or Luke? When Matthew and Luke deviate from Mark's order of episodes, why do they never do it in the exact same way? Such positive and negative considerations are usually called upon to make the case that Mark was the earliest Gospel and that Matthew and Luke used Mark independently.

Besides the material that they have in common with Mark, Matthew and Luke share a fairly large body of sayings and incidents not found in Mark at all. The material common to Matthew and Luke but absent from Mark is commonly designated by the symbol "Q." That symbol was first used in 1890 by Johannes Weiss as a cipher for the German word *Redenquelle* meaning "sayings-source." Q seems to have been a collection of sayings of Jesus (plus some other material) already in Greek form by the fifties of the first century A.D. It apparently contained no passion narrative. We have no written copy of Q. Its existence as a single document is a hypothesis, and whatever is said about it is necessarily hypothetical. Many books have been written in recent years about the text of Q and its theology, and one may legitimately wonder how these scholars determine what was in Q. They assume that we have Q material where Matthew and Luke coincide and Mark has nothing at all. When Matthew and Luke differ from one another slightly in such a case, then they try to explain the difference in the light of the author's unique editorial practices.

The views that Mark was the first Gospel to be written and that Matthew and Luke used both Mark and Q independently constitute the "Two-Document hypothesis." According to this hypothesis the relationships between the first three Gospels and the hypothetical sayings-source "Q" are to be diagramed in this way:

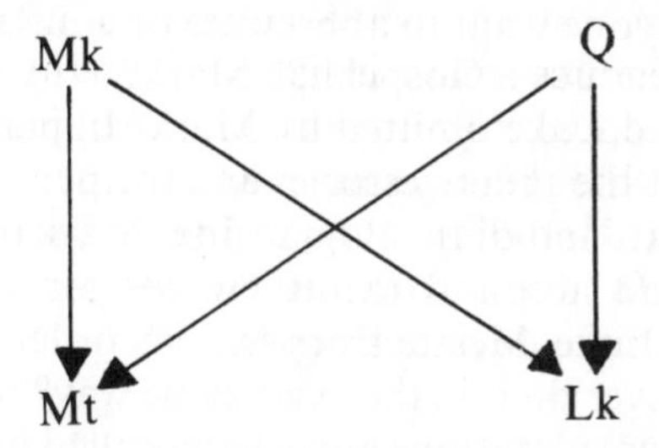


This hypothesis also leaves room for the use by Matthew and Luke of special material; that is, of traditions to which they alone of the Evangelists had access. These traditions usually are designated "M" and "L" respectively.

The most telling argument against this way of envisioning Synoptic relationships comes from the so-called "minor agreements" or small points in which Matthew and Luke agree with one another against Mark. According to the Two-Document hypothesis Matthew and Luke used Mark independently, and so they really ought not to agree in their modifications of Mark. Defenders of the Two Document hypothesis explain away these minor agreements in a variety of ways: (1) At some points Q may have overlapped with Mark, and here Matthew and Luke relied upon Q. (2) Matthew and Luke may have had access to a slightly different edition of Mark from what we have. (3) Those who copied the manuscripts may have harmonized the Matthean and Lukan texts. (4) Just as two competent teachers independently reading a student's paper will naturally introduce many of the same corrections, so Matthew and Luke are thought to have independently corrected Mark's rough Greek.

The Two-Document explanation of Synoptic relationships is a hypothesis; that is, an explanation of the phenomena asserted as a guide to investigation and accepted as highly probable in the light of established facts. No theory of Synoptic relationships including this one is absolutely unassailable. The Two-Document explanation is relatively simple and economical when compared with the other hypotheses. The vast majority of New Testament scholars today have accepted it as an adequate working hypothesis. Its usefulness has been confirmed by form-critical and redaction-critical studies. Its validity is assumed in the chapters that follow and in the Gospel commentaries of the New Testament Message series.

## *B. Examples of Source Criticism*

1. *Mark 1:2-3:* At the beginning of his Gospel, Mark introduces his treatment of John the Baptist with a quotation from the Old Testament:

> The beginning of the gospel of Jesus Christ, the Son of God.
> [2]As it is written in Isaiah the Prophet,
> "Behold, I send my messenger before thy face,
> who shall prepare thy way;
> [3]the voice of one crying in the wilderness:
> Prepare the way of the Lord,
> make his paths straight—"

Mark tells us that he is using a source—the book of the prophet Isaiah. The passage, which is cited in v.3, is from the beginning of the so-called Second Isaiah (chaps. 40—55) and describes the way back from the exile in Babylon to the land of Israel. The translation of the Hebrew text of Is 40:3 reads: "A voice cries: 'In the wilderness clear the way of Yahweh, make straight in the desert a highway for our God.'" The Septuagint Greek text is slightly different: "A voice of one crying in the wilderness: 'Prepare the way of the Lord, make straight the paths of our God.'" The text of Mk 1:3 is practically identical with the Septuagint Greek text except for the phrase "his paths" and seems to reflect the early church's application of the text to John as the precursor of Jesus and its identification of Jesus as the Lord.

The first part of the quotation, however, presents a real problem. Rather than being part of the book of Isaiah, it is usually described as a combination of Ex 23:20 and Mal 3:1. The Hebrew of Ex 23:20 reads: "Behold I am sending a messenger before you to guard you on the way and to bring you to the place that I have appointed." The Septuagint translates the passage in this way: "And behold I am sending my messenger before your face in order that he may guard you on the way so that he bring you into the land that I have prepared for you." The Hebrew of Mal 3:1 reads: "Behold I am sending my messenger, and he will clear a way before me." The Septuagint of this passage is: "Behold I send out my messenger, and he will look upon the way before me." It is hard to escape the impression that Ex 23:20 is being reused by the postexilic author of Malachi (500-450 B.C.) to describe the day of judgment when God will send some precursor.

Mk 1:2 uses Ex 23:20 for the first part ("behold I am sending my messenger before you") and Mal 3:1 for the second part ("who will look upon the way before me"). So in Mk 1:2 these two Old Testament quotations about a messenger are applied to John the Baptist and Jesus. The use of Mal 3:1 is especially important because of the traditional identification of John and Elijah (see Mal 4:5 where the messenger is described as Elijah) and because of its concern with the final age. The problem presented by Mk 1:2 is that by no stretch of the imagination can this verse be considered part of the book of Isaiah.

What source-critical conclusions can be drawn from Mark's use of Ex 23:20/Mal 3:1 and Is 40:3? Surely the Evangelist considered the Old Testament to be an authoritative source. Otherwise he would not have cited it at the very beginning of his treatment of John the Baptist. He seems to have used a Greek version of the Bible. There is little concern for the historical context of the Old Testament passages; the fulfillment of the Old Testament in the person of Jesus is considered far more important. The incorrect ascription of Ex 23:20/Mal 3:1 to the prophet Isaiah may indicate that the Evangelist used an anthology of biblical quotations applicable to Christ. Such anthologies of Old Testament quotations have been discovered among the Dead Sea scrolls. So Mark may well have had before his eyes the combination of Ex 23:20/Mal 3:1 and Is 40:3 in Greek in a collection of biblical quotations considered by early Christians as having been made perfectly intelligible with the coming of Christ.

The likelihood that Matthew and Luke used Mark's Gospel as a source allows us to trace the process still further. Both Matthew and Luke omit the Ex 23:20/Mal 3:1 part of the quotation. The Evangelists were probably aware independently of the problem created by the incorrect ascription and so in Mt 3:3 and Lk 3:4 they pass directly from the name of the prophet to the citation of Is 40:3. They correct Mark's mistake. Yet the Ex 23:20/Mal 3:1 passage does appear in both Gospels in connection with John the Baptist (Mt 1:10; Lk 7:26)—most likely a passage from Q, the non-Markan source used by both Matthew and Luke. This "minor agreement" of Matthew and Luke against Mark can be explained on the basis of the Two-Document hypothesis as reflecting (1) the independent corrections of an obvious error in the Markan source and (2) the overlap between Mark and Q.

2. *Jude 3-16/2 Peter 2:* That there is a relationship of literary dependence between Jude 3-16 and 2 Peter 2 is suggested first of all by the very similar content and structure of the two passages: a warning against the false teachers (Jude 3-4; 2 Pt 2:1-3), examples taken from the Old Testament tradition (Jude 5-7; 2 Pt 2:4-10a), and the denunciation of the opponents (Jude 8-16; 2 Pt 2:10b-22). Some very rare Greek words in the two denunciations also indicate that one author was copying from the other: "carouse together" (Jude 12; 2 Pt 2:13), "blemishes" (Jude 12; 2 Pt 2:13), "waterless" (Jude 12-13; 2 Pt 2:17), and "loud boasts" (Jude 16; 2 Pt 2:18). See also "scoffers" (Jude 18; 2 Pt 3:3).

Granted that there is a literary relationship between the two passages, can we decide which was the source and which was the revision? Several considerations regarding the Old Testament material make it more likely that Jude was the source for 2 Peter 2. The order of the Old Testament examples in Jude 5-7 seems haphazard: escape from Egypt and the destruction of the unfaithful Israelites (Exodus through Deuteronomy), the fall of the angels (Gen 6:1-4), and the punishment of Sodom and Gomorrah (Genesis 19). 2 Pt 2:4-10a flows according to the chronological order of the Old Testament: the fall of the angels (Gen 6:1-4), the flood (Gen 6:5-9), and the destruction of Sodom and Gomorrah (Genesis 19). Moreover, 2 Pt 2:4-10a develops the theme of God's mercy toward the righteous: "he preserved Noah, a herald of righteousness, with seven other persons" (v.5) and "he rescued righteous Lot" (v.7). It seems more reasonable to imagine that the author of 2 Peter has put the examples into their correct biblical order and has inserted the theme of God's mercy toward the righteous than to suppose that the author of Jude has scrambled the order of events and omitted the theme of compassion. Therefore Jude is most likely the source and 2 Peter the revision.

The use of "extracanonical" literature in Jude and its absence in 2 Peter 2 suggests that the reviser may have wished to impose on the text of Jude his own ideas about what is authoritative or canonical literature. The denunciation in Jude 8-16 cites five examples from the Jewish tradition: the archangel Michael (9), Cain (11), Balaam (11), Korah (11), and Enoch (14-15). 2 Pt 2:15-16 focuses upon the instances of Balaam's greed (see Numbers 22) and omits the other four. The omission of the Michael and Enoch incidents is especially significant. The dispute between the archangel Michael and the devil about Moses's body is not described in the Old Testament at all (see Deut 34:5-8) and is probably part of a Jewish writing called the Assumption of Moses. The quotation from Enoch in Jude 14-15 corresponds to the Greek version of 1 Enoch 1:9 and 60:8. Perhaps the author of 2 Peter wanted only one example instead of five. Yet the omission of these two extracanonical incidents does point to a more reserved attitude in 2 Peter toward what is an "authoritative" source and what is not. Thus the use of Jewish source material in Jude and 2 Peter 2 makes it likely that the former served as the literary source for the latter.

## *Bibliography: Source Criticism*

K. Aland (ed.), *Synopsis of the Four Gospels. Greek-English Edition of the Synopsis Quattuor Evangeliorum with the Text of the Revised Standard Version* (New York/London: United Bible Societies, 1978).

A. Huck and H. Greeven (eds.), *Synopsis of the First Three Gospels with the Addition of the Johannine Parallels* (13th rev. ed.; Tübingen: Mohr-Siebeck, 1981).

J.B. Orchard (ed.), *A Synopsis of the Four Gospels in a New Translation Arranged according to the Two-Gospel Hypothesis* (Macon, GA: Mercer University Press, 1982).

B.H. Throckmorton, Jr. (ed.), *Gospel Parallels. A Synopsis of the First Three Gospels* (4th rev. ed.; New York/ Nashville: Nelson, 1979).

---

A.J. Bellinzoni et al. (eds.), *The Two-Source Hypothesis. A Critical Appraisal* (Macon. GA: Mercer Universitv Press, 1985).

R.A. Edwards, *A Theology of Q. Eschatology, Prophecy, and Wisdom* (Philadelphia: Fortress, 1976).

W.R. Farmer, *The Synoptic Problem. A Critical Analysis* (rev. ed.; Dillsboro, NC: Western North Carolina Press, 1976).

I. Havener, *Q: The Sayings of Jesus* (Wilmington, DE: Glazier, 1987).

J.S. Kloppenberg, *The Formation of Q. Trajectories in Ancient Wisdom Collections* (Philadelphia: Fortress, 1987).

W.G. Kümmel, *Introduction to the New Testament* (tr. H.C. Kee; Nashville/New York: Abingdon, 1975) 38-80.

H.H. Stoldt, *History and Criticism of the Marcan Hypothesis* (Macon, GA: Mercer University Press, 1980).

C.M. Tuckett, *The Revival of the Griesbach Hypothesis. An Analysis and Appraisal* (Cambridge, UK—London—New York: Cambridge University Press, 1983).

# 6. FORM CRITICISM

## *A. Form Criticism in General*

LITERARY FORMS are the various modes of communication available to the writer and intelligible to the reader. They are part of our daily existence. For example, the daily mail may bring us a wedding invitation, an advertisement to subscribe to a magazine, and a letter from an old friend. Even by looking at the envelope or at the way in which we are addressed, we know almost instantly what is inside from its very form. Once the envelope has been opened, the physical disposition of the message will tell us even more. The wedding invitation will be nicely printed and written in a very elevated style, while the advertisement might be a mass-produced sheet beginning "Dear Sir or Madam." The personal letter may be handwritten, and its style will probably be informal and chatty. The fact is that we have at our disposal a wide range of conventional literary or oral forms, and the very form that we choose does a good deal of communicating on its own. If I want to get a job, I usually write up a resumé of my educational and work experience, and not a poem or a novel.

Literary forms change. If you looked at a newspaper from twenty years ago and compared it with today's paper, you would see that some things had remained pretty much the same; e.g., the form of the editorials, the advice column ("Dear Abby"), the obituary, the political cartoon. But the sports results are now presented so as to provide even more statistical information in a smaller amount of space.

The type-face used today may reflect developments in printing technology over the years. In the news stories the key female figures may no longer be identified as "Miss" or "Mrs.," or they may even be described as "Ms." One hundred years from now an observer who came upon part of today's newspaper with the date ripped off could rely on such external and purely formal features to say that it came from 1989 and not 1959.

In the study of Scripture, "form criticism" has both literary and historical purposes. Its literary task is to identify and understand the conventions by which the story of Jesus and the story of the early church were communicated. Its historical task is to get behind the large literary sources that might be identified (Mark, Q) as the earliest and to describe what was happening as the pre-literary traditions were handed on from person to person and community to community. The German term for the project *Formgeschichte*, which means "form history," expresses more effectively the literary and historical sides of this operation than the usual English term "form criticism" does.

Much of the early impetus for source criticism came from a desire to get back to the life and teaching of the earthly Jesus. The assumption was that if we could get back to the earliest written sources, then we could learn a good deal about the historical Jesus. But once having isolated Mark and Q as the earliest written sources, scholars then realized that these written sources had incorporated even older material. Mark did not compose his Gospel entirely out of his own head, but he seems to have had at his disposal some traditions about the deeds and teachings of Jesus. What was needed was a tool to get behind the earliest written documents and give us some insights into what was going on in the early churches that shaped this material about Jesus. Shortly after World War I three German New Testament scholars (K. L. Schmidt, M. Dibelius, and R. Bultmann) working independently applied form-critical techniques to the New Testament. Similar projects were underway in European literary criticism at the time (especially in classifying pieces of folklore), and form-critical work had already begun in Old Testament study under the influence of H. Gunkel. Most form-critical study of the Gospels since these initial probes has really been footnotes to the pioneering and still valuable work of Rudolf Bultmann.

Form criticism is the process of (1) discovering the original units of the tradition and (2) establishing the history of these units. In the case of the Synoptic Gospels form criticism moves from the existing text back to an earlier stage that no longer exists. That earlier stage consisted of discrete sayings and stories that can be classified by form. The traditions conveyed by those forms served the needs and purposes of the early church and had relevance to the internal and external problems confronting the Christian community. Analysis of these traditions can uncover the "setting in life" (*Sitz im Leben*) in which these traditions arose and were handed on. Form criticism is both a literary and a historical operation.

## *B. Discourse Forms in the Synoptic Gospels*

Instead of relying on two major examples as in the other chapters, I think it wise merely to explain briefly a number of literary forms found in the Synoptic Gospels. Since Bultmann's categories are so widely used, they can serve as our guide.

An *apothegm* is a saying set in a brief narrative. Mark 3:1-6 is an example:

> [1]Again he entered the synagogue, and a man was there who had a withered hand. [2]And they watched him, to see whether he would heal him on the sabbath, so that they might accuse him. [3]And he said to the man who had the withered hand, "Come here." [4]And he said to them, "Is it lawful on the sabbath to do good or to do harm, to save life or to kill?" But they were silent. [5]And he looked

> around at them with anger, grieved at their hardness of heart, and said to the man, "Stretch out your hand." He stretched it out, and his hand was restored. [6]The Pharisees went out, and immediately held counsel with the Herodians against him, how to destroy him.

The whole story revolves around the saying in v.4: "Is it lawful on the sabbath to do good or to do harm, to save life or to kill?" It is a piercing question that exposes the pettiness of the opponents and provides the justification for Jesus to heal on the sabbath. In a real sense the narrative functions as the vehicle for the saying, and one must at least reckon with the possibility that the saying once existed independently and that the story has been constructed merely to give it context.

What kind of community would have found this type of saying interesting and meaningful? Since sabbath observance would be of most interest to Jews and not to Gentiles, and since the Gospel of Mark was finally composed in large part for Gentile Christians (see Mk 7:3-4), it is unlikely that Mark would have invented a story that had so little meaning for his Gentile audience. The story revolves around the observance or nonobservance of the sabbath. That would have been an issue for the church in a heavily Jewish environment where Judaism set the cultural pattern and the early church had to explain its rather free attitude toward sabbath observance. This apothegm (and most others) probably reflects the debate between Palestinian Jews and Jewish Christians about the early church's practice and theology. The story serves to anchor the free attitude of the church regarding the sabbath in the teaching and example of the earthly Jesus.

A *proverb* is a brief saying expressing a general truth of a practical or a moral nature. A principle ("no man can serve two masters," Mt 6:24) expresses a truth of general experience and elicits the response "that's right!" An imperative expresses the truth in a command and expects obedience: "Do not be anxious about tomorrow, for tomorrow will be anxious for itself (Mt 6:34)." A question stimulates thought and urges the hearer to give an answer: "Which of you by being anxious can add one cubit to his span of life (Mt 6:27)?" Proverbs are so general and so common that they tell us little that is distinctive about the communities behind these teachings. They may have been used inside and outside the church to show Jesus as a great wisdom teacher, but it is hard to be more specific than this.

Among the other important discourse forms in the Synoptic tradition are *prophetic* and *apocalyptic sayings*: "Not everyone who says to me, 'Lord, Lord' shall enter the kingdom of heaven but he who does the will of my Father who is in heaven (Mt 7:21)." *Legal sayings* command or forbid certain kinds of action. The casuistic legal saying has the form "if/when . . . then." A case is described and a course of action is recommended: "When you give alms, sound no trumpet before you (Mt 6:2)." The apodictic legal saying is a simple command: "You shall not kill." The "I sayings" are statements in the first person singular about the name, origin, essence, status, or function of the person: "Think not that I have come to abolish the law and the prophets; I have not come to abolish them but to fulfill them (Mt 5:17)."

Form criticism obviously helps us to understand the literary character of the materials in the Synoptic tradition. The more of this literary character that we understand, the better we grasp the content. But as we have seen, Bultmann and others also used form criticism as an aid in reconstructing the early church's history. Bultmann divided early Christianity into two basic phases: Palestinian Christianity and Hellenistic Christianity. The Gospels as we have them are all in Greek and are presumably the product of the Hellenistic church. Yet there was an earlier phase in Palestine where Aramaic or Hebrew was the primary language. So, for instance, the apothegms probably reflect the life of the Palestinian church in defining itself against Judaism.

But there are problems connected with using form criticism as a historical tool. Pure form criticism claims to work independently of the content of the passage, but in practice (as in the case of the apothegm) the content seems to determine what is said about the form's history. Moreover, some of Bultmann's assumptions about the division between the Palestinian and Hellenistic churches and about the languages used in Palestine have been proven to be incorrect. Also, the degree of creativity that he attributed to the early church seems excessive to most New Testament scholars today. There simply does not seem to be enough hard evidence available to do what Bultmann tried to do in using form criticism as a means for reconstructing the history of the early church. Because it forces us to look at the devices used in the early church to communicate the good news, form criticism is a very useful literary tool. But its usefulness as a historical tool is open to much more question.

## *C. Narrative Forms in the Synoptic Gospels*

When we look at any of the canonical Gospels, what we see most clearly is a story or narrative about Jesus. The Gospels combine various forms (sayings, proverbs, etc.), but the integrating principle for the whole is the story of Jesus from his birth as in Matthew and Luke or from his baptism as in Mark or from eternity as in John, up to his death and resurrection. The story of Jesus' life is the fundamental principle of organizing the material in the Synoptic tradition.

The narrative seems to be intrinsically more interesting to human beings than other forms. Philosophical treatises, collections of sayings, factual reports, and chronicles are ways of communicating truth but nothing competes with stories. The narrative can include interesting details, can be told passionately, and remains in suspense until the story line is resolved. The narrative invites the audience to participate in what is being told, works on its emotions, and moves it to action. The narrative was particularly apt for a community grounding its faith in the living Christ; for the Evangelists, the Christ-event was not merely past history but also a living reality.

Part of the traditions from which our Gospels were formed consisted of short stories about Jesus. This is a very common way for groups focusing on an individual to remember their hero. Around Boston people frequently tell anecdotes about John F. Kennedy or the legendary Mayor James Michael Curley. Form criticism insists that such stories follow certain patterns, contain certain elements, and adhere to certain rules. The two most important types of narratives in the Synoptic Gospels are healings and nature miracles.

A *healing story* is a narrative about a powerful person who is able to restore the health of one previously in a state of sickness. The healing comes about by more than natural means and is viewed as but a sample of the healer's power. Mark 1:40-45 is a good example of a healing story:

> [40]And a leper came to him beseeching him, and kneeling said to him, "If you will, you can make me clean." [41]Moved with pity, he stretched out his hand and touched him, and said to him. "I will; be clean." [42]And immediately the leprosy left him, and he was made clean. [43]And he sternly charged him, and sent him away at once, [44]and said to him, "See that you say nothing to any one; but go, show yourself to the priest, and offer for your cleansing what Moses commanded, for a proof to the people." [45]But he went out and began to talk freely about it, and to spread the news, so that Jesus could no longer openly enter a town, but was out in the country; and people came to him from every quarter.

The term used to describe the sick man ("a leper") in v.40 would have had dramatic and fearful overtones, much as "cancer" does in the twentieth century. Palestinian Jews knew that the skin diseases constituting "leprosy" (not identical with modern Hansen's disease) involved ritual uncleanness and segregation from the community. There was no need for a lengthy description to establish the seriousness of the case. All the elements of v.40 (beseeching, kneeling, requesting) bring out the leper's utter dependence upon the power of Jesus and suggest that he could not be healed by natural means. Vv.41-42 describe the healing action. The personal interaction between Jesus and the leper is concretized by a healing touch and a healing word. Some kind of "ritual" of healing is quite common in these stories. By stating that "immediately the leprosy left him" the narrator insists that the healing was due to Jesus' power alone, and not to natural processes over a long stretch of time. Vv.43-45 provide (or look forward to) proof from a third party that the healing had really occurred. Usually the proof is simply the amazement of the crowd, but in the case of leprosy the most effective and official proof would be the testimony of the priests (see Leviticus 13). The major elements in the healing story are the description of the sick person's condition (Mk 1:40), the healing action (Mk 1:41-42), and the testimony of some third party (Mk 1:43-45). None of this is very surprising, since any account of healing naturally involves diagnosis, therapy, and restoration to health. In the early church the stories about Jesus' healing powers would have consoled and encouraged Christians in their distress or need, for Jesus could be approached as an instrument of God's power. Such stories also would have contributed to the high opinion of Jesus as a powerful figure. They would have been recounted in homilies and exhortations in the church and in debate with the adversaries of Christianity.

A *nature miracle* is a narrative in which the powerful hero transcends the laws of nature to perform some helpful action. The stilling of the storm in Mark 4:35-41 is a good example:

> [35]On that day, when evening had come, he said to them, "Let us go across to the other side." [36]And leaving the crowd, they took him with them, just as he was, in

> the boat. And other boats were with him. [37]And a great storm of wind arose, and the waves beat into the boat, so that the boat was already filling. [38]But he was in the stern, asleep on the cushion; and they woke him and said to him, "Teacher, do you not care if we perish?" [39]And he awoke and rebuked the wind, and said to the sea, "Peace! Be still!" And the wind ceased, and there was a great calm. [40]He said to them, "Why are you afraid? Have you no faith?" [41]And they were filled with awe, and said to one another, "Who then is this, that even wind and sea obey him?"

Vv.35-36 provide a narrative bridge from the parables in Mark 4 and serve to get Jesus into the boat and the midst of the storm. The reference to "other boats" is an odd detail never taken up in the present story and may be the remnant of an earlier form of the account. Vv.37-38 describe the menace of the elements: a great storm of wind, waves beating the boat, the boat in danger of capsizing, and the panic of the disciples. It is possible that the perils of the storm at sea might have had theological overtones and might have pointed to Jesus' identity. In the ancient Near East and the Old Testament creation is frequently depicted as a contest between the supreme God (Yahweh) and the forces of chaos and evil represented by a storm at sea. It is hard to estimate how much (if any) of this was intelligible to people in Jesus' time. V.39 describes the calming action performed by Jesus. The storm is portrayed in almost personal terms as something to be addressed and rebuked, and the "great calm" shows the contrast between the menacing condition of the storm and what happened as a result of Jesus' intervention. The reaction of the disciples in vv.40-41 is one of awe and puzzlement about who Jesus really is. So this nature miracle has a general structure not unlike that of the healing story: the menace of the elements (vv.37-38), the act of power (v.39), and the response of wonder (vv.40-41). A story such as this would have provided the early Christians with consolation and encouragement regarding the power of Jesus. It would have led them also to ask, "Who then is this?"

## *D. Parables in the Synoptic Tradition*

Biblical scholarship over the past sixty years has emphasized the importance of the parables as reflecting Jesus' preaching of the kingdom of God, and has tried to establish that many of the parables can be attributed with some certainty to the earthly Jesus. The parable combines aspects of discourse and narrative. Matthew 13:31-33 presents two stories—about the mustard seed and the leaven respectively—that are explicitly labelled as parables in the biblical text itself:

> [31]Another parable he put before them, saying, "The kingdom of heaven is like a grain of mustard seed which a man took and sowed in his field; [32]it is the smallest of all seeds, but when it has grown it is the greatest of shrubs and becomes a tree, so that the birds of the air come and make nests in its branches."
>
> [33]He told them another parable. "The kingdom of heaven is like leaven which a woman took and hid in three measures of meal, till it was all leavened."

Both purport to teach something about the mysterious entity called "the kingdom of heaven." Both use the expression "is like" and then proceed to tell a story that would be readily intelligible to people familiar with mustard seeds and the process of making bread. Both are simple and uncomplicated, told without extraneous details.

The British scholar C. H. Dodd defined the parable in this way: "a metaphor or simile drawn from nature or common life, arresting the hearer by its vividness or strangeness, and leaving the mind in sufficient doubt about its precise application to tease it into active thought." So in Mt 13:31-32 the interesting case of the small mustard seed becoming a large tree tells us something about the coming of the kingdom of heaven. And in Mt 13:33 we hear about a small amount of leaven which transforms a whole batch of flour into a large quantity of dough and thereby tells us something about the coming of the kingdom of heaven. The interesting cases are provided by the mustard seed and the leaven. The real subject matter is the coming of the kingdom of heaven. The feature for comparison is the sure but sudden transformation that occurs. According to Bultmann's categories, the parable is a kind of comparison or similitude. He constructs a spectrum of figurative speech in which the parable has a central position: figure (e.g., Mt 7:9-10), pure similitude (Lk 17:7-10), parable (Lk 15:11-32), example story (Lk 10:30-35), and allegory (Mk 12:1-9). These distinctions are not all hard and fast, but they do indicate the wide variety of comparative materials in the Synoptic tradition.

The parables in the Gospels exhibit some important formal techniques of good story telling. They are concise and economical in describing events and actions. They use direct speech (dialogue) or soliloquy to increase vividness. They rely on repetition to build up patterns and then call upon contrast or antithesis to underline the real point. The punch line is saved to the end, and it comes as something of a surprise. The details in the narrative are generally in the service of a single point. Though there are obvious allegorical features in some parables, the attempt to treat the parables as allegories and to work out one-for-one correspondences (A "stands for" Z, B "stands for" Y, etc.) is doomed to failure and involves a serious misunderstanding of the parable as a literary form.

This discussion of parables began with the observation that they seem to reflect a characteristic method of teaching used by the earthly Jesus. If that is so (and there is no good reason to deny it), then the parables in our Gospels must be read and interpreted at three different levels: the life of Jesus, the life of the early church, and the Gospel itself. At each level a different set of questions is appropriate. At the "Jesus" level we want to ask: How does the parable reflect Jesus' preaching of the kingdom of God? At the "church" level we are interested in how and why the parable was preserved and what need or function it served in the earliest community. At the "Gospel" level we want to know why the Evangelist included it where he did and how its positioning furthered his literary and theological purposes.

## *E. Forms in Other Parts of the New Testament*

The fact that this discussion of literary forms in the New Testament has focused on the Synoptic Gospels should not give the impression that only in them is form criticism important. On the contrary, it is just as significant to recognize and analyze the literary forms used by John and Paul and the rest of the biblical authors as it is in studying the works of the Synoptic Evangelists. Even a cursory glance at John's Gospel will illustrate the point. The Fourth Gospel begins with what seems to be an adaptation of a hymn (1:1-18), recounts a series of "signs" or miracles that Jesus performed (2:1-11; 4:46-54; 5:1-9; 6:1-14; 6:15-25; 9:1-8; 11:1-45; and perhaps 21:1-14), uses dialogue very often, and presents long speeches in which Jesus reveals his identity and his relationship to the Father. The farewell discourse of Jesus in John 17 has been called a "testament," and the Gospel reaches its climax in the intricately designed trial narrative before Pilate in Jn 18:28—19:16.

Besides the gospel the other prominent larger form or literary genre in the New Testament is the epistle. Sometimes the terms "letter" and "epistle" are used to mark the extreme ends of a spectrum. According to this convention "letter" refers to the personal communication between two individuals or between an individual and a group, while "epistle" is a formal treatise on a topic and is designed for general publication. Though this distinction is artificial and is seldom observed, it does make the point that the canon contains a wide variety of epistolary communications ranging from more or less personal letters (Philemon and 3 John) through advice for specific communities (1-2 Corinthians) to epistolary treatises (Hebrews, James, 1 John).

The letters in the New Testament use many of the formal conventions of the ancient letter. They customarily begin by identifying the sender ("Paul") and the recipients ("to the saints at Rome"), and present a salutation ("grace and peace"). This pattern is frequently embellished with uniquely Christian titles and phrases ("called to be apostle"), but the three-element framework of sender, recipient, and salutation remains constant. Then a thanksgiving follows: "I give thanks to God always for you . . . ." These introductory features were as much a part of the ancient letter form as our address and date/addressee/salutation ("Dear ____") are part of the modern epistolary convention. The New Testament letters also end on a conventional note with advice about conduct (paraenesis) and instructions to convey personal greetings to individuals within the community. It is not at all surprising that Paul and the other New Testament letter writers should adhere to the epistolary conventions of their time and express their message by means of and within them. But twentieth-century readers who are unaware of or disregard these conventions in their study of the New Testament epistles run the risk of serious misunderstanding.

Even the main part or "body" of the New Testament letters frequently includes smaller standard literary forms. We have studied some of these already. Romans 11:33-36 ("O the depth of the riches and wisdom and knowledge of God! . . .") is a doxology in which God's attributes are celebrated. 1 Corinthians 15:3b-5 ("Christ died for our sins in accordance with the scriptures, . . .") is a kerygmatic formula; that is, a brief summary of the Christian message.

Philippians 2:6-11 ("who, though he was in the form of God, did not count equality with God a thing to be grasped . . .") is a pre-Pauline hymn. Other hymnic fragments in the NT are to be found in Col 1:15-20; Eph 2:14-16; 1 Tim 3:16; Heb 1:3; and Jn 1:1-18. Another form is the catalogue of vices exemplified by Gal 5:19-21: "Now the works of the flesh are plain: immorality, impurity, licentiousness, idolatry, sorcery, enmity, strife, jealousy, anger, selfishness, dissension, party spirit, envy, drunkenness, carousing, and the like." The household code (*Haustafel* in German) in Col 3:18—4:1 (see also Eph 5:21—6:9; 1 Pt 2:18—3:7) describes the responsibilities of husbands, wives, children, masters, and servants. These are but a few of the many smaller literary forms that Paul and other New Testament authors had at their disposal and used in their attempts to communicate the good news to people in the first century A.D.

## *Bibliography: Form Criticism*

R. Bultmann, *The History of the Synoptic Tradition* (tr. J. Marsh; Oxford: Blackwell, 1963).

M. Dibelius, *From Tradition to Gospel* (tr. B. L. Woolf; New York: Charles Scribner's Sons, 1934).

W. G. Doty, *Letters in Primitive Christianity* (Guides to Biblical Scholarship, New Testament Series; Philadelphia: Fortress, 1973).

J. Jeremias, *The Parables of Jesus* (tr. S. H. Hooke; rev. ed.; New York: Charles Scribner's Sons, 1963).

J. Lambrecht, *Once More Astonished. The Parables of Jesus* (New York: Crossroad, 1981).

G. Lohfink, *The Bible: Now I Get It! A Form-Criticism Handbook* (Garden City, New York: Doubleday, 1979).

E. V. McKnight, *What Is Form Criticism*? (Guides to Biblical Scholarship, New Testament Series; Philadelphia: Fortress, 1969).

R.H. Stein, *An Introduction to the Parables of Jesus* (Philadelphia: Westminster, 1981).

# 7. HISTORICAL CRITICISM

## *A. Historical Criticism and the Gospels*

IN THE DISCUSSION of form criticism the question of the relationship between the Synoptic tradition and Jesus came into focus. According to most critical New Testament scholars today, there is a gap of forty to sixty years between Jesus' death in A.D. 30 and the composition of the Gospels in their present forms (see Appendix One). Despite the claims of some early Christian writers, it is very doubtful that any of the Evangelists was an eyewitness to the events described in their Gospels. Matthew and Luke used written sources (Mark and Q), and Mark seems to have had existing blocks of material about Jesus. The most certainty that we have concerns the final form of the Gospels. In other words, we can say quite confidently that the Evangelists believed such and such about Jesus. In the period between Jesus' death and the composition of the Gospels the traditions about Jesus' deeds and teachings were handed on in the church and were probably modified somewhat according to the church's needs and problems. That is the domain of form criticism. As we move back from the life of the church to the life of Jesus, certainty is even harder to attain.

What really happened? Historical criticism studies a narrative purporting to convey historical information in order to determine what actually occurred in so far as this is possible. This is no easy task even in our own days. Sifting through the various accounts of John F. Kennedy's assassination in 1963 in order to say "what really happened" on that day in Dallas ends in confusion and bewilderment for many people. The many versions of the Watergate affair do not answer all our questions about what really happened and why. If it is so difficult to sort out what happened in such recent events in a culture that puts a great deal of emphasis on "hard facts," how much the more difficult is it to say what "really happened" in Palestine almost two thousand years ago!

The Synoptic Gospels present some peculiar problems to those who must know what really happened. Sometimes the same events are described in different ways, as in the story of the stilling of the storm (Mk 4:35-41 and Mt 9:18-27) discussed in the preceding and the next chapters. To say that the Evangelists were describing two different events or to harmonize the accounts into one long account are tactics of desperation. No, the same event is being described but in different ways; or rather, as we will see, Matthew seems to have rewritten Mark's account from his own perspective. But did Jesus really still the storm solely by the power of his word? If he did, why did not some historian of the period like Josephus or Tacitus find out about it? Or are we simply dealing with a symbolic account (an "epiphany") in which according to early Christian imagination Jesus is revealed as the Lord of the natural elements?

Even the most skeptical reader of the Gospels has to admit that Jesus performed extraordinary acts of healing. The oldest traditions in the Synoptic Gospels (e.g., Mt 11:21-22 and Lk 11:20) connect Jesus' exorcisms and healings with his preaching of the kingdom of God. His opponents (see Mk 3:22) admit his unusual powers, and the rabbinic descriptions of him as a sorcerer and deceiver allude to his abilities as a miracle worker. The narration of these acts of healing follows the threefold pattern of the obstacle to be removed, the healing process, and the response of amazement confirming the miracle. But there are some distinctive features to Jesus' healings. Far from being exhibitions or displays, they usually respond to genuine human needs and teach something about the kingdom of

God. Generally Jesus acts by means of his own power without explicit recourse to his Father in prayer. Most of Jesus' miracles are healings and present little problem for most people, though the terms in which they might be described may differ (e.g., as psychosomatic healings, as magic, as divine power). The historical critic can penetrate through the Gospel accounts to say with some confidence that Jesus really healed certain individuals.

The "nature miracles" like the stilling of the storm, however, present some special problems. The "nature miracles" are displays of power in which the so-called "laws of nature" are violated. In the Gospels the most important nature miracles are the multiplication of the loaves and fishes, the changing of water into wine, the walking on the water, the withering of the fig tree, and the stilling of the storm. In evaluating these accounts several factors must be considered: The nature miracles are relatively few in number. They usually occur only in the presence of the disciples. The accounts have many allusions to the Old Testament. They are not singled out in the summaries of Jesus' activities (see Mk 1:32-34; 3:10-12; etc.). How you as a historical critic deal with such incidents really depends not on the methods of exegesis that are described in this book but rather on the philosophical mindset that you bring to the text. That observation applies whether you are a total skeptic or a fundamentalist or anything in between.

How much can we know about the earthly Jesus, as a historical figure before his death in A.D. 30? There are some serious obstacles in our way. Our concerns with exact and scientific historiography are very different from the concerns of the Gospel writers. As much as the Gospels might look like biographies, they really are documents of faith reflecting the beliefs and interests of the early Christians as well as the life of Jesus. We can evolve a general outline of Jesus' life from the Gospels: He was raised in Nazareth, baptized by John the Baptist, exercised a ministry of preaching and healing, went up to Jerusalem, and was crucified there. But the chronological framework of the Gospels does not enable us to go much further in writing a biography of Jesus. Whatever Matthew and Luke have of chronological information is derived from Mark, since Q had little or no chronology attached to it. Mark himself was putting together blocks of tradition according to his own theological lights, and his framework of a one-year ministry and one visit to Jerusalem is probably less accurate historically than John's schema of a three-year ministry and several trips to Jerusalem.

What can we know about Jesus' teaching? The problem here is trying to distinguish between the teaching of Jesus and the possible modifications and adaptations of it by the early church. Some useful criteria for making such distinctions have been evolved: (1) dissimilarity or discontinuity; that is, a saying that is so unique that it cannot be ascribed to contemporary Judaism or to the early church may be ascribed to Jesus; (2) multiple attestation; that is, if a specific teaching is ascribed to Jesus in several independent traditions (Mk, Q, M, L, John, Paul), it probably can be attributed to Jesus; (3) Palestinian coloring; that is, if a teaching only makes sense when translated back into Aramaic or Hebrew or reflects the life and customs of Palestine in Jesus' time, then it is at least possible to ascribe it to Jesus who spoke Aramaic and lived in Palestine; (4) coherence; that is, if a teaching coheres with or is consistent with teachings attributed to Jesus by the other criteria, it may well be an authentic teaching of Jesus.

One does not have to be a genius to perceive that these criteria are somewhat shaky: (1) The criterion of dissimilarity or discontinuity gratuitously assumes a separation of Jesus from his environment and from the movement that he inspired. It implies that much more is known about Judaism in Jesus' time than is actually known. Finally it may tell us what is unique about Jesus' teaching but not necessarily what was central or characteristic in his teaching. (2) The criterion of multiple attestation has to reckon with the possibility that all the sources go back to some early Christian prophet speaking in Jesus' name and not to Jesus at all. (3) The criterion of Palestinian coloring has to reckon with the fact that before and after Jesus' death and resurrection his first followers still spoke Aramaic and remained in Palestine. (4) The criterion of coherence stands or falls with the other criteria.

Whatever logical problems these criteria involve, the practical application of them to the teaching materials in the Gospels does tell us something about the teaching of the earthly Jesus. Jesus preached the coming of God's kingdom in the future and the inauguration of it in his own life and ministry. He taught and acted out of a deep concern for the poor, for sinners, for women, and for other disadvantaged groups. He had a free attitude toward the Pharisaic tradition about the observance of the Law and perhaps even toward the Law itself. His prayers and teachings about God imply a special relationship with the Father—a relationship that he had and wished to share with his disciples. In his acts of healing he took the initiative and displayed his own power.

Nevertheless, we have to admit that the early church may well have attributed material to Jesus, and so we have an obligation to search out the dynamics of this process in so far as is possible. But at the same time we should be sensitive to the continuities between Jesus and the church. For example, there is a continuity between Jesus' practice of sharing meals with outcasts and the church's celebration of the Eucharist. There is also a continuity between Jesus' questioning attitude toward Judaism and the church's final definition of itself as not a sect within Judaism but as open to those outside of Israel. Finally and most importantly, the Evangelists wrote their Gospels precisely to anchor the faith and identity of the Christian community in the person of Jesus of Nazareth.

We must be careful to respect the peculiar character of the Gospels and the complexity that interpretation of them necessarily involves. Practically speaking, we must avoid the extremes of fundamentalism ("if the text says, Jesus said, that is enough for me") and skepticism ("we can know nothing about the earthly Jesus"). Neither attitude is justified. The peculiar character of the Gospels brings home to us the nature of early Christianity as a movement or a process. The Gospels are privileged witnesses to the interaction between the person of Jesus and the faith of the believing community, an interaction that continues and in which we as Christians still participate today.

## *B. Examples of Historical Criticism*

1. *Mark 14:58:* In his portrayal of the "trial" of Jesus (Mk 14:55-66), Mark (or his source) seems bent on presenting the preliminary investigation held the evening *before* the first day of Passover, according to the Johannine passion narrative, as a full-scale trial before the Jewish Sanhedrin or council *on* the first day of Passover. According to Mark there were two charges levelled against Jesus: Jesus threatened to destroy the Temple (14:58) and made messianic claims with political overtones (14:62). The first of these charges illustrates some of the concerns of historical criticism: "We have heard him say, 'I will destroy this temple that is made with hands, and in three days I will build another, not made with hands.'"

Jesus' prophecy about the Temple has a good claim to authenticity since it cannot be readily derived from Judaism or the early church and since it is consistent with Jesus' activity. The combination of the destruction and restoration of the Temple in a single saying is unique in the Jewish tradition. It is not easily derived from Christianity after A.D. 70, since by then the Romans (and not Jesus) had destroyed the temple at Jerusalem and no new Temple had been erected. The saying also satisfies the criterion of multiple attestation. In Mk 14:58; Mt 26:61; and Acts 6:14 it is used by the opponents as ammunition against Jesus. The tendency to "spiritualize" the saying and adapt it to the post-A.D. 70 situation can be seen in Mt 26:61: "This fellow said, 'I *am able* to destroy the temple of God, and to build it in three days.'" In Acts 6:14 it is connected with a change in Jewish customs: "for we have heard him (that is, Stephen) say that this Jesus of Nazareth will destroy this place, and will change the customs which Moses delivered to us." In Jn 2:19-21 ("destroy this temple, and in three days I will raise it up") it occurs at the very beginning of Jesus' ministry and is interpreted as a prophecy of the resurrection ("he spoke of the temple of his body").

In addition to satisfying the criteria of dissimilarity and multiple attestation, the Temple saying seems to reflect a Palestinian background. Passover was a pilgrimage feast in which pious Jews from all over the world were supposed to come up to Jerusalem. Herod the Great had begun an extensive rebuilding program on the Jerusalem Temple (see Jn 2:20) with the result that this construction project employed thousands of people and had become a major industry. But there seems to have been some opposition on the part of people from rural sections of Palestine to Herod's venture. It had been started by a non-Jew by birth (Herod was an Idumean), incorporated "foreign" or Hellenistic architectural features, solidified and increased the power of the high priests and elders, and brought about more religious commercialization. At a pilgrimage feast like Passover, which celebrated the simple origins of Jewish piety, such hostility toward the Temple would naturally be intensified. Jesus' saying about the Temple may well have been interpreted by the authorities as a call to sabotage the building operations. Even the simple folk of Jerusalem whose economic well-being was connected with the building project at the Temple would have viewed Jesus as a serious threat to their livelihood. In short, Jesus' saying about destroying the Temple fits in with the opposition of the rural population of Palestine toward the building of Jerusalem Temple initiated by Herod the Great.

Is the Temple saying consistent with what we know of Jesus? The cleansing of the Jerusalem Temple (Mk 11:15-19; Mt 21:12-13; Lk 19:45-48; Jn 2:13-22) is a well-attested prophetic action undertaken by Jesus, and the Temple saying probably had some connection with it. In the context of Jesus' apocalyptic preaching about the kingdom of God, the Temple saying could well have been the symbolic expression of Jesus' hopes for the new age. In the coming kingdom, religion as it is presently constituted (represented by the cult at the Jerusalem Temple) will pass away. After the kingdom comes ("in three days" being an Old Testament way of describing a decisive change), a new way of worshiping God will emerge. Jesus may have been uttering this saying in the name of God or perhaps even expressing his own pivotal role in the history of salvation. In the setting of the Passover pilgrimage both the authorities of the Jerusalem Temple and the Roman officials would have viewed such a statement with great suspicion. They would have supposed that Jesus was yet another Jewish political-messianic pretender and so would have taken steps to silence him.

2. *Galatians 1:11-17/Acts 9:1-19; 22:3-21; 26:9-18:* Galatia in Asia Minor (modern Turkey) was a place to which Paul brought Christianity, but in a very short time (by the mid-fifties of the first century A.D.) the predominantly Gentile-Christian community there had become infatuated with a more "Jewish" kind of Christianity. The situation infuriated Paul who looked upon this infatuation as a betrayal of the true gospel. In order to instruct the Galatians Paul wrote them a very strong letter in which he omitted the customary thanksgiving and went straight to the point: "I am astonished that you are so quickly deserting him who called you in the grace of Christ and turning to a different gospel" (Gal 1:6). Then in an effort to establish the divine origin of the gospel that he had taught the Galatians, Paul in Gal 1:11-17 described his former life in Judaism and his new life in Christ:

> [11]For I would have you know, brethren, that the gospel which was preached by me is not man's gospel. [12]For I did not receive it from man, nor was I taught it, but it came

> through a revelation of Jesus Christ. [13]For you have heard of my former life in Judaism, how I persecuted the church of God violently and tried to destroy it; [14]and I advanced in Judaism beyond many of my own age among my people, so extremely zealous was I for the traditions of my fathers. [15]But when he who had set me apart before I was born, and had called me through his grace, [16]was pleased to reveal his Son to me, in order that I might preach him among the Gentiles, I did not confer with flesh and blood, [17]nor did I go up to Jerusalem to those who were apostles before me, but I went away into Arabia; and again I returned to Damascus.

This autobiographical description of Paul's "conversion" is paralleled by three accounts in the Acts of the Apostles (9:1-19; 22:3-21; 26:9-18). The historical critic is concerned with sifting through these four accounts in the hope of determining (in so far as this is possible) what "really happened." Clearly Paul's own statements about his experience can serve as a reliable criterion for what happened, and the accounts in Acts can be judged according to their conformity or disagreement with his first-person narrative.

Where Gal 1:11-17 and the accounts in Acts agree, we can be quite sure that reliable historical traditions were used. Paul's confession that he had persecuted the church of God violently (Gal 1:13) is a prominent theme in all three Acts accounts (see especially 26:9-11) and is hardly the kind of thing that early Christians would have invented about him. His boast to have reached an advanced stage in Judaism and to have been very zealous (1:14) is paralleled in Acts 22:3 and 26:4-5. The connection between the vocation of Paul and his mission to preach the gospel to the Gentiles is drawn in both Gal 1:16 and Acts 26:16. Finally, Gal 1:17 ("and again I returned to Damascus") indirectly connects the incident with Damascus, though we are not told that it occurred on the way to Damascus as in the Acts accounts. There are certainly enough similarities here to conclude that the Acts accounts reflect some good historical traditions going back to the personal experience of the apostle Paul.

Did Luke get his information about the so-called Damascus experience directly from Paul? The apparent disagreements between Gal 1:11-17 and the Acts accounts suggest that he did not. Nothing in Paul's own writings indicates that he was the kind of person who would have gone into the detail of the Lukan narratives about his own calling. In Gal 1:16 he is satisfied with "was pleased to reveal his Son to me." Furthermore, Luke leaves undecided the question as to how Paul saw Christ. The light and the voice (see Acts 9:3-4; 22:6-7; 26:13-14) are mysterious in origin and perhaps consciously blurry. The reason for this conscious blurriness may well be Luke's desire to set Paul's experience apart from the experiences that the apostles had of the risen Lord in Lk 24:13-53 before the ascension. Whereas for Paul (according to 1 Cor 15:3-9) these experiences were of the same kind, Luke distinguished the apostles who were eyewitnesses of the earthly Jesus (see Acts 1:21-26) from apostles like Paul and Barnabas (see Acts 14:4,14) who were not. Finally, in Gal 1:11-12 the gospel and presumably the mission attached to it come directly in the revelation, but in Acts 9 and 22 Paul learns what God planned for him through the agency of Ananias. The conclusion drawn by G. Lohfink in his *The Conversion of St. Paul: Narrative and History in Acts* (Chicago: Franciscan Herald, 1976) seems to explain the situation quite accurately: "The report in Acts is not an exact verbal transcript of what really happened, yet it certainly is not pure fiction either. Rather it is both a report of a well attested historical tradition (cf. the Pauline letters) as well as Luke's interpretation and explanation of this historical tradition presented in conventionally accepted literary forms and literary techniques" (p. 101).

## *Bibliography: Historical Criticism*

G. Bornkamm, *Jesus of Nazareth* (New York: Harper & Row, 1960).
A.E. Harvey, *Jesus and the Constraints of History* (Philadelphia: Westminster, 1982).
R.A. Horsley, *Jesus and the Spiral of Violence. Popular Jewish Resistance in Roman Palestine* (San Francisco: Harper & Row, 1987).
J. Jeremias, *New Testament Theology. The Proclamation of Jesus* (New York: Charles Scribner's Sons, 1971).
H.C. Kee, *Miracle in the Early Christian World. A Study in Sociohistorical Method* (New Haven—London: Yale University Press, 1983).
B.F. Meyer. *The Aims of Jesus* (London: SCM, 1979).
N. Perrin, *Rediscovering the Teaching of Jesus* (New York/ Evanston: Harper & Row, 1967).
J. Riches, *Jesus and the Transformation of Judaism* (London: Darton, Longmann & Todd, 1980).
E.P. Sanders, *Jesus and Judaism* (Philadelphia: Fortress, 1985).
A. Schweitzer, *The Quest of the Historical Jesus. A Critical Study of its Progress from Reimarus to Wrede* (tr. W. Montgomery; New York: Macmillan, 1959).
G. Theissen, *The Miracle Stories of the Early Christian Tradition* (Philadelphia: Fortress, 1983).
G. Vermes, *Jesus the Jew. A Historian's Reading of the Gospels* (New York: Macmillan, 1974).
A. Weiser, *The Miracles of Jesus Then and Now* (tr. D.L. Tiede; Herald Biblical Booklets; Chicago: Franciscan Herald, 1972).

# 8. REDACTION CRITICISM

## *A. Principles of Redaction Criticism*

THE WORD "redaction" in the phrase "redaction criticism" is a rare item in English. According to the dictionary, "to redact" means "to draw into suitable literary form, revise, or edit." Clearly the term may be unusual but the operation is a very familiar one. If you have ever served as the recording secretary at a meeting, your work in organizing what the participants said and in producing a final report was an exercise in "redaction." If you have ever been asked to take a written proposal and improve upon it, your act of redrafting the motion was an exercise in redaction. If you have ever been asked to rewrite someone else's report and add to it important information that had been omitted, your rewriting was an exercise in redaction. Redaction criticism proceeds from the realization that the New Testament writers' choice of material, the order in which they placed what they had collected, and the alterations they made in the traditional material were determined to some extent by their theological outlooks. The redaction critic wants to know why the gathering and ordering of various traditions have led to this particular form of a Gospel or Epistle. The redaction critic wants to know what these traditional materials meant for the biblical writer and for the community in which he lived and for which he wrote, and why they have been modified.

Redaction criticism is obviously the child of source criticism and form criticism. As we saw in our discussion of source criticism, one of the major factors inspiring it was the hope of getting accurate knowledge about the earthly Jesus. Source criticism had established that the Gospel of Mark was very likely the earliest Gospel and was used independently by Matthew and Luke. Redaction criticism would naturally be interested in the ways in which Matthew and Luke used their sources—what they chose to include or omit, the order in which they presented the material, and the changes that they introduced. These adaptations would tell us a good deal about what Matthew and Luke thought and what crises they were confronting. But source criticism also established that even Mark had sources before him. Far from writing a chronicle of Jesus' life, Mark reshaped traditional materials in the light of his own special interests such as the secret identity of Jesus the Messiah and the disciples' lack of understanding. By isolating the traditional materials available to the Evangelists (including Mark), the form critics set the stage for the redaction critics. But strangely enough the form critics viewed the Evangelists primarily as collectors and editors, and they paid surprisingly little attention to the theological significance involved in the redactional process.

Though individual scholars had practiced redaction criticism from time to time, it was only after World War II that it became an established and explicit method for interpreting New Testament texts. In 1948 Günther Bornkamm wrote a brief article on the story of the stilling of the storm in Mt 8:18-27. He showed how Matthew took over the story told in Mk 4:35-41 and reinterpreted it as a paradigm of Christian discipleship. Later Bornkamm and two of his students (G. Barth and H. J. Held) presented a comprehensive examination of Matthew's redactional practices and theological concerns. In 1954 Hans Conzelmann presented a full-scale study of Luke's theology in which he isolated some of the Evangelist's major emphases. For example, Luke's interest in Jerusalem as the place of the resurrection appearances of Jesus was seen to have some connection with the city's role as the place from which the good news went forth. Also, Conzelmann discerned a three-stage view of salvation history operative in Luke-Acts: the time of Israel (including John the Baptist), the time of Jesus' ministry, and the time of the church. In 1956 Willi Marxsen published a study of Mark's Gospel in which he coined the term "redaction criticism." The application of redaction criticism to Mark is somewhat more hypothetical than it is to Matthew or Luke where it is relatively easier to see what the Evangelist was doing with his sources. Since these pioneering efforts, redaction criticism has been applied to practically every part of the New Testament with quite remarkable results.

The questions asked by the redaction critic are fairly obvious ones. Assuming that the sources available to the biblical writer can be determined with some accuracy, the redaction critic is interested first and foremost in the unique views or unusual emphases that the biblical writer placed upon the sources at his disposal. Once having gained some familiarity with these unique views or unusual emphases, the redaction critic is then interested in the setting in life or life situation in which the biblical writer functioned and in the theological purpose or purposes of the final composition. Once more the German term *Redaktionsgeschichte* ("redaction history") is more expressive of the literary and historical tasks of the process than the customary English designation "redaction criticism." So the redaction critic has two fundamental questions: (1) What unique views or unusual emphases does the author place on the source? (2) What is the author's life situation and theological outlook?

Although redaction criticism is the child of source criticism and form criticism, attention to the sharp differences between form criticism and redaction criticism may contribute something to our understanding of both. Form criticism and redaction criticism begin by trying to distinguish between traditional material and editorial material. In other words, source criticism is the necessary first step in each procedure. Form criticism concentrates on the pre-literary tradition and ignores the redaction, while redaction criticism focuses on the redaction and sets aside the tradition. Form criticism sees the Evangelists largely as collectors and transmitters of traditions, while redaction criticism looks upon them as authors in their own right. Form criticism is mostly concerned with the small units constituting the tradition, while redaction criticism is concerned with the larger units formed out of the smaller blocks and the achievement of producing a whole Gospel or a whole Epistle. Form criticism is occupied with the various life situations in the early church in which the material has been used and modified, while redaction criticism focuses on the final author's life situation and his theological purposes. These are generalizations and are subject to some modification, but they do get across the basic point that form criticism has to do with the pre-literary stage of the documents and redaction criticism deals with the final product.

Redaction criticism has emerged as a very popular and significant way to approach the study of the New Testament. If we grant the reliability of source criticism especially as applied to the Synoptic Gospels, redaction criticism enables us to deal with something very specific. It allows us to see what at least one early Christian writer made of the existing tradition. In the case of the Gospels it enables us to grasp better the achievements of the Evangelists as transmitters of tradition and its interpreters, as theologians in their own right. Finally, redaction criticism gives us an insight into the history of Christianity in the first century and shows us how the church took its place in the world and faced issues like apostasy, internal squabblings, waning enthusiasm, and persecution.

Redaction criticism has proved its value in practice, but there are still some serious problems connected with it. Redaction critics sometimes go to excess in carrying out their task. Over-theologizing, allegorizing, and psychologizing are the major pitfalls encountered as they try to speak about the theological purposes and achievements of the New Testament writers. In the case of the Synoptic Gospels redaction criticism has generally worked on the assumption of the Two-Document hypothesis (see above, Source Criticism, pp. 61-64). Only a few scholars have tried to do redaction criticism on the basis of an alternate source hypothesis, though some have tried to proceed without resorting to any source hypothesis at all. But, as we saw previously, there is no utterly unassailable solution to the Synoptic problem. If the Two-Document hypothesis were ever definitely refuted (an unlikely prospect), then most of the redaction-critical studies of the Gospels would have to be redone. Furthermore, in the material peculiar to Matthew (M) or Luke (L) it is difficult to distinguish between tradition and redaction. Yet that is an important distinction for the redaction critic, who wants to know what the Evangelist transmitted and what he may have composed on his own. Finally, by focusing on the unique views or unusual emphases of the redactor the redaction critic runs the risk of ignoring the tradition being transmitted. The redactor himself may well have thought that the content of the tradition was the most important matter imaginable and that his own editorial retouches were of minor significance. All these issues are serious theoretical problems, but the following examples will show that redaction criticism has indeed proved itself in practice.

## *B. Examples of Redaction Criticism*

1. *Matthew 8:18-27:* In the chapter on form criticism the story of the stilling of the storm in Mk 4:35-41 was cited as an example of a nature miracle. Jesus shows himself as the powerful lord and master even of the elements of nature in putting down the storm. In their amazement the disciples can only ask: "Who then is this, that even wind and sea obey him?" The Markan account of the stilling of the storm is focused primarily on the identity of Jesus.

In chapters 8 and 9 of his Gospel, Matthew presents nine (or ten) acts of power done by Jesus. By placing these stories directly after Jesus' Sermon on the Mount (chapters 5 through 7) the point is made that the Jesus who is powerful in word (the "Sermon on the Mount" of Mt 5—7) is also powerful in deed (Mt 8—9). In 8:18-27 Matthew has re-written Mark's account and given it a second focus—the theme of discipleship. By comparing Matthew's version with Mark's, we can see in some detail the unique views and unusual emphases that he has placed on his Markan source:

Mk 4:35-41

> [35]On that day, when evening had come, he said to them, "Let us go across to the other side." [36]And leaving the crowd, they took him with them, just as he was, in the boat. And other boats were with him. [37]And a great storm of wind arose, and the waves beat into the boat, so that the boat was already filling. [38]But he was in the stern, asleep on the cushion; and they woke him and said to him, "Teacher, do you not care if we perish?" [39]And he awoke and rebuked the wind, and said to the sea, "Peace! Be still!" And the wind ceased, and there was a great calm. [40]He said to them, "Why are you afraid? Have you no faith?" [41]And they were filled with awe, and said to one another, "Who then is this, that even wind and sea obey him?"

Mt 8:18-27

> [18]Now when Jesus saw great crowds around him, he gave orders to go over to the other side. [19]And a scribe came up and said to him, "Teacher, I will follow you wherever you go." [20]And Jesus said to him, "Foxes have holes, and birds of the air have nests; but the Son of man has nowhere to lay his head." [21]Another of the disciples said to him, "Lord, let me first go and bury my father." [22]But Jesus said to him, "Follow me, and leave the dead to bury their own dead."

> [23]And when he got into the boat, his disciples followed him. [24]And behold, there arose a great storm on the sea, so that the boat was being swamped by the waves; but he was asleep. [25]And they went and woke him, saying, "Save, Lord; we are perishing." [26]And he said to them, "Why are you afraid, O men of little faith?" Then he rose and rebuked the winds and the sea; and there was a great calm. [27]And the men marveled, saying, "What sort of man is this, that even winds and sea obey him?"

The first major change appears in Mt 8:18. Whereas in Mk 4:35 Jesus made a suggestion ("let us go across to the other side"), in Mt 8:18 "he gave orders" to go over to the other side. This difference obviously serves to highlight the authority of Jesus and to show that he is fully in charge from the start. The next major change comes in Mt 8:19-22. Matthew has taken two sayings about discipleship from the Q tradition (see Lk 9:57-62) and placed them in the story of the stilling of the storm. Both sayings describe people who want to be disciples of Jesus. In the first case (Mt 8:19-20) Jesus warns his prospective followers not to expect personal security since he himself ("the Son of man") has none. In the second case (Mt 8:21-22) he insists that discipleship involves a total commitment and is even more important than the very sacred obligation of seeing to the burial of one's father. By insisting that Jesus is in command ("he gave orders") and by inserting these sayings about discipleship, Matthew makes it clear that this narrative is not simply about the stilling of a storm. No, it is also a story about following Jesus.

In Mt 8:23 the action resumes with Jesus fully in command. Whereas in Mk 4:36 the disciples are said to have taken Jesus with them, in Mt 8:23 their role is described by means of "follow" used as a technical term for discipleship: "his disciples followed him." Once again the theme of discipleship is underscored. Mk 4:36 also contains a very peculiar statement: "and other boats were with him." The statement is peculiar because, as the story proceeds, nothing is said about the other boats and the boat occupied by Jesus and his disciples seems to be the only one affected by the storm. As a careful editor Matthew perceived this as an unnecessary and extraneous detail and so omitted it altogether. Mark's description of the storm in 4:37-38 is quite vivid: "And a great storm of wind arose, and the waves beat into the boat, so that the boat was already filling. But he was in the stern, asleep on the cushion. . . ." Again Matthew seems to have regarded some of these details as dispensable, and so his own description in 8:24 is a scaled down version: "And behold, there arose a great storm on the sea, so that the boat was being swamped by the waves; but he was asleep." So Mt 8:23-24 reveals two facets of the Evangelist's redactional technique: his continuing interest in the theological theme of discipleship and his editorial tendency to omit what he perceives to be extraneous details.

The disciples' request to Jesus to do something about their safety is very different in the two Gospels. In Mk 4:38 they say: "Teacher, do you not care if we perish?" But Matthew in 8:25 has them use terms that in the early church would have been familiar in prayer: "Save, Lord; we are perishing." The words "save" and "perish" referred not merely to the physical side of human existence but had also taken on the spiritual overtones of salvation and damnation. Furthermore, to call upon Jesus as "Lord" was to use the language of prayer. So in their distress the disciples address Jesus in a prayer of petition.

Matthew has straightened out the order of events in the story. In Mk 4:38-40 the disciples make their request; Jesus awakens; he calms the sea; and he criticizes the disciples for their lack of faith. But how could Jesus hear their request if he were still asleep? So in Mt 8:25 the disciples wake Jesus and then make their request. In Mt 8:26 Jesus first criticizes the disciples for their "little faith" and then calms the sea. The change from "have you no faith?" (Mk 4:40) to "men of little faith" (Mt 8:26) is significant. Throughout his Gospel Mark presents a somewhat negative picture of Jesus' first followers. Time after time they misunderstand who Jesus is and what he is doing; at his passion and death they lose their nerve entirely. The description of them as having "no faith" at all is not inaccurate. But Matthew is careful to upgrade the image of the disciples, and he prefers to use the expression "little faith" here and elsewhere to place them in a middle ground between having no faith at all and having perfect faith in the risen Lord.

Some of Matthew's modifications of the Markan account of the stilling of the storm are simply the kind of changes that a careful editor would naturally introduce; e.g., omitting extraneous details and smoothing out the order of events. At some points Matthew seems to be making even more explicit themes that are underdeveloped or only implicit in the Markan text; e.g., the authority of Jesus and the disciples' relationship to him. In both narratives Jesus is the powerful Lord who is able to control the elements, but Matthew with the petition "save, Lord; we are perishing" in 8:25 adds the idea that in times of distress Christians may pray to Jesus as the powerful Lord. Besides the theme of Jesus' lordship Matthew has given the story a new focus—the theme of discipleship.

So much for Matthew's unique views and unusual emphases in rewriting the story of the stilling of the storm. But what does this analysis of Matthew's redactional achievements tell us about his life situation? Of course, one must be very cautious about building up a whole scenario for the Matthean community out of one passage. But redaction-critical analyses of other passages in the Gospel have revealed that Matthew's community was confronting some serious problems. A detailed study of chapter 13 led J. D. Kingsbury to list these issues: materialism, secularism, spiritual slothfulness, hatred among Christians, lovelessness, apostasy, and lawlessness. From his study of Mt 17:22—18:35, W. G. Thompson concluded that Matthew's community was badly divided, scandal was a threat (18:5-9), and the need for fraternal correction was urgent (18:15-20). In its troubled situation the most significant resort for the community of Jesus' disciples (the church) was prayer to him as their powerful Lord. That would explain the twin emphasis in Mt 8:18-27 on Jesus' extraordinary power and discipleship. In the face of the storm within it and around it, the Matthean community is urged to stand beside the first followers of Jesus and call out: "Save, Lord; we are perishing." For further details, see G. Bornkamm in *Tradition and Interpretation in Matthew*, pp. 52-57.

2. *1 Timothy 3:14-16:* In the middle of 1 Timothy we meet a verse that proposes to summarize the mystery of our religion (v.16):

> [14]I hope to come to you soon, but I am writing these instructions to you so that, [15]if I am delayed, you may know how one ought to behave in the household of God, which is the church of the living God, the pillar and bulwark of the truth. [16]Great indeed, we confess, is the mystery of our religion:
> He was manifested in the flesh,
> vindicated in the Spirit,
> seen by angels,
> preached among the nations,
> believed on in the world,
> taken up in glory.

The way in which that verse is introduced and the radical differences in its language and style from the material surrounding it suggest that it existed before 1 Timothy did. In other words 1 Tim 3:16 seems to reflect the use of a source. The source material is structured on the basis of antithetic parallelism: flesh-spirit, angels-nations, and world-glory. The Greek text is characterized by a certain rhythmic quality and by assonance. All these features indicate that the source cited in 1 Tim 3:16 was probably part of a hymn according to which Christ (1) took on human flesh (incarnation) and was vindicated in the resurrection, (2) was given worship by the angelic powers and preached among peoples even outside of Israel, and (3) accepted in the world of human affairs and exalted to heaven.

How has the author of 1 Timothy used this source? There is little reason to suppose that he has tampered with the wording of the hymnic fragment at all. Once having isolated the source, the redaction critic is then primarily interested in how the hymnic fragment has been woven into the document in which it now stands. 1 Timothy is a collection of warnings and church regulations, and 3:14-16 is really the hinge of the whole letter in that it provides the theological basis for the warnings and rules. V.15 describes the church as "the household of God" and "the pillar and bulwark of the truth." To give content to what is meant by the word "truth" in this context, the author cites part of a Christian hymn—something that presumably was already familiar to the readers.

What was the life situation in which 1 Timothy arose? Most interpreters today view the Pastoral Epistles (1 and 2 Timothy and Titus) as having been composed not by Paul but rather by a disciple or an admirer of Paul late in the first century A.D. (see Appendix One). The church at this point was defining itself over against other institutions in society and was also laying down rules for Christian conduct and for offices within the church. The late first-century church was threatened by certain exotic religious currents both within and outside the Christian community. Part of the strategy in this situation was to insist on the significance of the church and its officials as guardian of the deposit of faith. Another part of the strategy was to appeal to established formulas of faith. See also 1 Tim 1:17; 6:15-16; 2 Tim 2:11-12. Both facets are illustrated in 1 Tim 3:15-16 by the way in which the church is described and by the citation of the hymnic fragment.

## *Bibliography: Redaction Criticism*

G. Bornkamm, G. Barth, and H. J. Held, *Tradition and Interpretation in Matthew* (tr. P. Scott; Philadelphia: Westminster, 1963).

H. Conzelmann, *The Theology of Saint Luke* (tr. G. Buswell; New York: Harper & Row, 1961).

J. L. Martyn, *History and Theology in the Fourth Gospel* (New York / Evanston: Harper & Row, 1968).

W. Marxsen, *Mark the Evangelist. Studies of the Redaction History of the Gospel* (tr. J. Boyce et al.; Nashville / New York: Abingdon, 1969).

N. Perrin, *What Is Redaction Criticism?* (Guides to Biblical Scholarship, New Testament Series; Philadelphia: Fortress, 1969).

# 9. PARALLELS

## *A. Using Literary Parallels*

IT IS IMPORTANT to distinguish a literary source from a literary parallel. The use of a source involves the direct literary dependence of one text upon another. In other words, author B had possession of the writing by author A and copied or adapted it. But in geometry "parallel" lines by definition never meet. Rather, they proceed to infinity, equidistant one from another. In literature a parallel involves some point or points of similarity between two texts where direct literary dependence is unlikely or not proved. Parallels to New Testament texts can be taken from any body of literature and from any period of history. A hymn from the twentieth century could conceivably illumine the hymn preserved in Phil 2:6-11, or the fate of an apocalyptic movement active today in the South Sea Islands might tell us something about the development of the early church. But the most important parallels in biblical studies are those that come from documents roughly contemporary with the New Testament and from intellectual and religious movements that inhabited the same social world—the Roman empire—as the early church did. Comparison of biblical passages with Jewish and pagan texts can provide valuable information about language and literary style, the literary forms and genres, and the motifs and patterns of thought. This in turn enables the modern reader to enter more deeply into the world of the New Testament and understand these writings in somewhat the same way that their original readers did. In short, study of these parallels in works from the same time and culture as the New Testament can tell us what was "in the air."

The first step in dealing with a literary parallel involves taking an inventory of similarities and of differences between the two texts. What elements do the two texts being compared have in common, and at what points do they differ or contradict one another? Fifty zeroes still add up to zero, and so the interpreter must be careful to assess the strength or weakness of the supposed parallels. The second step is concerned with the historical relationship existing between the two texts. A quotation from Plato may be very like a specific New Testament text, but a similar saying found in the book of Wisdom (a Jewish book composed in the first century B.C. and showing Greek philosophical influences) is obviously more relevant to the interpretation of the New Testament. So the second question to be asked in examining a literary parallel is this: What is the historical relationship between the two texts? Assuming that there is no direct literary dependence between the two texts and so there is no question of the use of a source, we want to rely upon materials that are the most likely to reflect the social setting in which early Christianity developed. Since early Christianity was first and foremost a Jewish movement, we ought to know something about Jewish history from Alexander the Great to A.D. 100 and about the primary sources available to those who wish to investigate literary parallels to the New Testament.

## *B. Jewish History from Alexander the Great to A.D. 100*

By 323 B.C. Alexander's conquest of the eastern Mediterranean world was complete. That means that for some three hundred and fifty years before the time of Jesus' public ministry Palestine was open to and influenced by the trends of Greek culture. After Alexander's death his empire was divided among his generals and friends, and from this time on Palestine became a battleground between the Seleucids based in Syria and the Ptolemies based in Egypt. For about one hundred and sixty years Jewish history in Palestine was dominated by attempts on the part of these two dynasties to gain control of it. From 300 B.C. to 200 B.C. the Ptolemies had the upper hand, but from 198 B.C. until 167 B.C. the Seleucids had the upper hand.

The Seleucid emperor Antiochus IV Epiphanes (175-163 B.C.) conquered Egypt and sought to bring Palestine more completely into his sphere of cultural dominance. Antiochus was trying to make his own brand of Hellenistic culture the pattern for all the peoples of his empire. In 167 B.C. he profaned the temple at Jerusalem by setting up another cult. This sparked off a native Jewish revolt led by a priestly family from outside of Jerusalem under the father named Mattathias. The members of the family gained the nickname of "Maccabees" or "hammers." The Maccabean revolt was successful because it mobilized local resistance to the Seleucids and won the support of the Romans whose power was rapidly increasing during the mid-second century B.C.

Ironically the Jewish dynasty that stemmed from the Maccabees (also called the Hasmoneans) probably did more to impose Hellenistic culture in Palestine than Antiochus IV Epiphanes ever did. Simon (143-134 B.C.), the oldest son of Mattathias, united to himself the roles of general, high priest and political ruler, but his boldness stirred up the criticism of conservative elements which had originally supported the Maccabean revolution. John Hyrcanus I (134-104 B.C.) conquered the Samaritans and destroyed their temple in 128 and also incorporated Idumea (ancient Edom) into his kingdom. Alexander Jannaeus (104-77 B.C.) was imprisoned for a brief period by his brother Aristobulus I who reigned for a short time. Alexander was released, won political control, and exercised leadership for a quarter of a century. At his death his wife Alexandra (77-67 B.C.)

took over the political power and was very favorable to the Pharisees. Since Alexandra as a woman could not be the high priest during her reign as queen, she appointed John Hyrcanus II to that office. But when she died, others supported the claims of Aristobulus II to the office of high priest. In 63 B.C. the Roman general Pompey entered Jerusalem by force and settled the dispute in favor of John Hyrcanus II. This action meant that the Jewish high priest and political-military ruler was now directly responsible to the Romans and that Rome had the role of arbiter of disputes in Palestine.

While these disputes about the high priesthood were taking place, the influence of Antipater the Idumean was steadily growing in Jerusalem. Idumea had been annexed to Palestine in the time of John Hyrcanus I, and now its leader was beginning to play a significant role in Jewish affairs. Antipater was appointed procurator of Judea by the Romans, while John Hyrcanus II was named ethnarch but had power only in the religious sphere. Antipater's son Herod (37-4 B.C.) married the granddaughter of the Jewish high priest and so reunited in himself and his family the powers exercised by the Maccabees. A skilled politician, Herod spent his reign playing one Roman faction off against the other and managed not only to survive but also to carry out a massive building program.

After Herod's death in 4 B.C., his kingdom was divided among his surviving sons. The best known son was Herod Antipas who ruled in Galilee until A.D. 36 and plays a role in the Gospel accounts of the deaths of John the Baptist and Jesus. The other well-known son was Archelaus who ruled Judea from 4 B.C. to A.D. 6. But things had become unstable and even chaotic in Jerusalem by A.D. 6, and so the Romans began to appoint a series of governors or procurators. From A.D. 6 to 44 there was relative stability in Judea due to the policies of the emperors Augustus and Tiberius and to the continuous tenure of the Ananus family as high priests. The most turbulent and most famous time in this period was the rule of Pontius Pilate (A.D. 26-36) when Jesus was put to death. A series of controversial Roman procurators from A.D. 44 to 66 and a vacuum in the local leadership led to a full-scale revolt in A.D. 66.

In May of 66 anti-Roman riots broke out in Caesarea Maritima and Jerusalem, and sacrifices on behalf of the emperor ceased in June. The leaders of the rebellion were some aristocratic patriots from Jerusalem and Zealots from Galilee. Between 67 and 69 the general Vespasian conquered Galilee, Perea, and western Judea, and he occupied the outskirts of Jerusalem before he was named the Roman emperor on July 1 of A.D. 69. His son Titus succeeded Vespasian as general of the army in Palestine and in A.D. 70 besieged Jerusalem from April to August. Finally on August 10 the temple at Jerusalem was captured and burned. After A.D. 70 the Jews in Palestine lost their political independence and their right to political self-determination. The Jewish council or Sanhedrin ceased to function, and the temple-services came to an end.

The significance of the destruction of the temple cannot be overestimated. The spiritual and political center of Judaism had been destroyed, and without its temple Judaism had to be constituted in a different way from before 70. This was the achievement of the rabbis who carried on the impetus provided by the founding of the academy at Yavneh (or Jamnia) by Yohanan ben Zakkai. These monumental events also contributed to the fact that the Christians no longer understood themselves as a sect within Judaism but rather as a new religious entity. Practically all the books of the New Testament, except Paul's letters, were put into final form after the destruction of the Jerusalem temple (see Appendix One).

During the time from Alexander to A.D. 100 Jews also lived in places other than Palestine. At the turn of the common era the total Jewish population of the Roman empire outside of Palestine and of the Parthian empire (including the Jewish community of Babylonia) considerably exceeded the number of Jews living in their homeland. A number of factors had inspired Jews to take up residence in the so-called Diaspora: expulsion, political difficulties, religious conflicts, and tempting economic prospects in new countries. The major centers of Jewish population outside of Palestine were Alexandria in Egypt, Antioch in Syria, Damascus, Babylonia, and Rome. With the exception of Alexandria we have little or nothing that we can say is the literary product of any of these sites, but the synagogues in most of these cities were the bases from which the Christian missionaries began their preaching of the gospel and won some of their first converts.

## *C. Primary Sources for Literary Parallels to the New Testament*

Christianity began as a Jewish movement. Jesus was a Jew. His first disciples were Jews. The earliest converts to Christianity were mostly Jews or Gentiles already sympathetic to Judaism. All the authors of New Testament books with the possible exception of Luke seem to have been Jews. Therefore it stands to reason that the extrabiblical literature which will shed the most light on early Christianity is the Jewish literature used or written between 100 B.C. and A.D. 100. What writings are available from this period?

The importance of the collection of Jewish writings that we call the Old Testament cannot be overestimated during the period. Whether or not it is appropriate to speak of the canon of the Old Testament at this time is debatable, but the fact that these books were considered authoritative writings is clear from practically every page of the New Testament and from every other contemporary Jewish work. People in Jesus' time were very much concerned with interpreting and actualizing their religious heritage. The Apocrypha or Deuterocanonicals are books included in the canon of the Greek and Latin Bible (and so in the Catholic canon of the Old Testament) but are not present in the Hebrew Bible (which equals the Jewish and Protestant canons). The most important books among the so-called Apocrypha are 1 and 2 Maccabees, Ecclesiasticus or Sirach, Wisdom, Judith, Baruch, and Tobit. English translations of them can be found in almost all the editions of the Bible being published today, whether they are under Catholic or Protestant auspices.

The term "Pseudepigrapha" ("written under a false name") is usually applied to those noncanonical Jewish writings from Jesus' time other than the Apocrypha. The title arises from the fact that many of these works were put forth under the names of great figures from the Old Testament. The most important Pseudepigrapha are Jubilees, 1 Enoch, Testaments of the Twelve Patriarchs, Assumption of Moses, 2 Baruch, 4 Ezra, Psalms of Solomon, 4 Maccabees, and Pseudo-Philo's Biblical Antiquities. At present the Pseudepigrapha are available in English in the collections edited by R.H. Charles, H.F.D. Sparks, and J.H. Charlesworth (the most extensive and up-to-date). It is often difficult to be precise about the time and place of origin of the individual Apocrypha and Pseudepigrapha, but these difficulties are offset to some degree by the content and the religious sentiments expressed in these books. They are precious witnesses to the religious variety within Judaism around the time of Jesus.

The Dead Sea scrolls were discovered in 1947 at Qumran, a site not far from Jerusalem. These documents are the literary remains of a Jewish religious movement which flourished from the middle of the second century B.C. to A.D. 70. Some of the scrolls are the documents of the sect itself (Rule of the Community, War Scroll, Thanksgiving Hymns, and Damascus Document) that allow us to see how an eschatologically-oriented Jewish movement roughly contemporary with the early church understood itself and structured itself. Among the scrolls the oldest known texts of the Old Testament have been found. Not only have these discoveries given us Hebrew biblical texts a thousand years older than what had been available prior to 1947, but they also have allowed us to see at first hand the variety of the types of biblical texts in use at the time of Jesus. The Dead Sea scrolls also include paraphrases of biblical stories (Genesis Apocryphon), line-by-line interpretations (Pesher on Habakkuk), targums (Targum of Job), pseudepigraphical books (Jubilees, 1 Enoch), and liturgical fragments. Several one-volume English translations of the Dead Sea scrolls (by G. Vermes, A. Dupont-Sommer, and T. H. Gaster) are available.

Josephus was a Palestinian Jewish general who went over to the Roman side during the revolt of A.D. 66-70. His major literary works were published in Greek. The *Jewish War* is a detailed description of the events leading up to the revolt and of the revolt itself, and the *Jewish Antiquities* describes the history of the Jews from Adam down to the Jewish War. Josephus is important because he preserved and transmitted traditional interpretations of various Old Testament passages and because his accounts of Jewish life at the turn of the Christian era are the most extensive sources available.

Philo, who was roughly speaking a contemporary of Jesus, was a prominent figure in the Alexandrian Jewish community. His allegorical commentaries on the Old Testament show how the Bible could be harmonized with the philosophical currents of the Hellenistic world. The Loeb Classical Library series presents on facing pages the Greek texts and English translations of the extant writings of Josephus and Philo.

Judaism in Jesus' time was largely an oral culture. But around A.D. 200 an attempt was made to bring together the laws, customs, biblical interpretations, and maxims into a compilation called the Mishnah. The compilation of traditions left out of the Mishnah is called the Tosefta, and the Palestinian Talmud (ca. A.D. 400) and the Babylonian Talmud (ca. A.D. 500) are commentaries on the Mishnah. The Targums are Aramaic translations and paraphrases of the Hebrew Bible. These so-called rabbinic writings provide precious information about the life and customs of the Jewish people. But the major problem in using them in New Testament research is obvious: How can we be sure that the traditions contained in these books have anything to do with Judaism prior to A.D. 70?

Greek and Roman pagan writings are also significant in New Testament study. The biblical authors wrote in Greek, and so comparison with the writings of their contemporaries can shed light on the language and literary forms used in the Scriptures. Furthermore, writers like Plutarch and Lucian describe in some detail the religious beliefs and rituals of the pagan cults that were the chief rivals of early Christianity outside of Palestine. The writings are also to be found in the Loeb Classical Library series.

In late 1945 the remains of a monastery library were discovered in Nag Hammadi in Egypt. The library consists of Coptic writings dating from the fourth century A.D., but these are really translations of Greek works that reflect the intellectual and religious movement called gnosticism. Previously gnosticism had been known primarily from the attacks against it on the part of early Christian writers such as Irenaeus. Now the primary source material for the gnostic movement is available in *The Nag Hammadi Library in English* (1977) edited by James M. Robinson. Gnosticism emerges as a very old movement, perhaps even earlier than Christianity. In fact some of the religious currents within the church that were challenged by Paul and other New Testament authors may well have been gnostic in orientation. But the problem encountered in using these documents in New Testament study is similar to that encountered in the case of the rabbinic writings: How can we be sure that the gnosticism of these fourth-century Coptic documents reflects the gnosticism that may have troubled the early church?

## *D. Examples of Literary Parallels*

1. *Mark 1:4-8:* Early in his Gospel Mark provides a description of the personality and activity of John the Baptist:

> [4]John the baptizer appeared in the wilderness, preaching a baptism of repentance for the forgiveness of sins. [5]And there went out to him all the country of Judea, and all the people of Jerusalem; and they were baptized by him in the river Jordan, confessing their sins. [6]Now John was clothed with camel's hair, and had a leather girdle around his waist, and ate locusts and wild honey. [7]And he preached, saying, "After me comes he who is mightier than I, the thong of whose sandals I am not worthy to stoop down and untie. [8]I have baptized you with water; but he will baptize you with the Holy Spirit."

The passage tells us that John preached that sinners should be baptized or immersed in water as a sign of their repentance, that he attracted great crowds from Jerusalem and all over Judea, that he dressed as the prophet Elijah did (see 2 Kgs 1:8, "he wore a garment of haircloth, with a girdle of leather about his loins"), and that he contrasted his own baptism with that of one "who is mightier than I."

The Jewish historian Josephus describes John the Baptist in Antiquities 18:116-119. He says that John was a good man who exhorted the Jews to practice justice toward their fellows and piety toward God. The rite of baptism is described as "a consecration of the body implying that the soul was already thoroughly cleansed by right behavior." So great were the crowds which John gathered around him that Herod Antipas began to suspect him of stirring up a rebellion. Herod Antipas then had him killed because he considered John to be a political threat.

What points do these passages have in common? Both Mark and Josephus present John the Baptist as a preacher of repentance, as using the rite of baptism in connection with the forgiveness of sins, as attracting great crowds, and as having been killed by Herod Antipas (see Mk 6:14-29). Where do the texts differ? Josephus gives no description of John's clothing and diet (compare Mk 1:6) and does not tell us much about the religious content of John's preaching (compare Mk 1:7-8). Josephus is content to represent John as a moral teacher who "exhorted the Jews to lead righteous lives, to practice justice towards their fellows and piety towards God." Moreover, Mark in 6:14-29 traces John's execution to his fearless indictment of the moral character of Herod Antipas while Josephus explains it from the political standpoint that Herod feared John's growing influence over the masses.

There is no reason to suppose that Josephus used Mark's account or that Mark used Josephus' account. We are dealing with parallels, not sources. This kind of comparison tells us some important things about Mark's Gospel and about Josephus' Antiquities. Mark emphasizes John the Baptist as a prophetic figure after the pattern of Elijah and as a preacher of the coming kingdom of God. The placing of the description at the beginning of the story of Jesus shows that John's relation to Jesus is another Markan concern. Josephus' presentation passes over the nuances of John's preaching and activity and focuses on his political significance—something fully in keeping with the purposes and interests of Josephus' political-military history. Mark wrote Christian religious history, and Josephus wrote political-military history.

2. *John 1:1:* Perhaps the most famous verse in the entire New Testament appears at the very beginning of John's Gospel: "In the beginning was the Word, and the Word was with God, and the Word was God." Jesus is identified as the revealer and the revelation of God. The passage asks us to reflect on our efforts to speak a word and to apply that process to the relation between the Father and Jesus. Imagine God, the all powerful creator and sustainer of us all, thinking and getting an idea that would communicate to all creation what was most distinctive and divine about him.

Imagine God wishing to reveal himself to people. According to the prologue of John's Gospel, God has done precisely this in the person of Jesus. The word that he has chosen to speak is Jesus, and that very word shares in the divinity.

The quest for parallels to the presentation of Jesus as the Word of God covers most of the range of primary sources described above. In the Old Testament the "word of the Lord" has a certain energy of its own (Jer 1:2; 20:8; Is 40:8; 55:10-11), and Wisdom 9:1 praises God for having made all things "by thy word." Following the descriptions of Wisdom as a personal figure in Proverbs 8—9, several of the Apocrypha develop (perhaps in response to the Egyptian cult of Isis) the themes of Wisdom's preexistence, personal attributes, and search for a home. In Sirach 24 the proper dwelling place for Wisdom is Jerusalem, and Wisdom itself is equated with "the book of the covenant of the Most High God" (v.23). In Wisdom 7:25-27 the figure is described in Hellenistic philosophical terms: "a breath of the power of God, and a pure emanation of the glory of the Almighty . . . a reflection of eternal light, a spotless mirror of the working of God, and an image of his goodness." 1 Enoch 42:2 describes Wisdom's vain search for a home: "Wisdom went forth to make her dwelling place among the children of men, and found no dwelling place. Wisdom returned to her place and took her seat among the angels." The parallel between this text and Jn 1:11 is especially striking: "He came to his own home, and his own people received him not."

Philo of Alexandria speaks frequently of the "word" of God in the sense of a created intermediary between God and his creatures. The *logos* (the Greek term for "word") was the entity that gives meaning and structure to the universe and to the individual person, but it did not have personal qualities nor was it preexistent. The rabbinic writings follow Sirach 24 in identifying Wisdom and the Law and speak of the Law as preexistent and as supplying the blueprint for creation. The Targums use the Aramaic word *mêmrā'* as a surrogate for God or the divine presence, and that term means "word."

The search for parallels to the "Word" in Jn 1:1 leads beyond the boundaries of Judaism. The sixth-century B.C. philosopher Heraclitus described the word (*logos*) as the eternal principle of order within the universe. The Stoic philosophers viewed the word of God as the mind of God guiding and directing all things. The gnostic Gospel of Truth 16:34-36 speaks of "the power of the Word that came forth from the pleroma—the one who is in the thought and the mind of the Father." Even the cult of the Egyptian goddess Isis must be considered. In this popular religious movement, which had adherents all over the Roman empire, the attributes of the goddess singled out for praise are strikingly similar to the Jewish descriptions of the person of Wisdom and hence to the Johannine portrayal of Jesus as the Word of God. In fact, the Jewish personification of Wisdom may well be in reaction to the popularity of the Isis cult.

None of these texts is so close to what we find in Jn 1:1-18 that we must consider it to be in a direct relationship of literary dependence. In other words, there is no reason to think that the Evangelist had before him the book of Sirach, or the writings of Philo, or the praises of Isis. Rather, he was apparently picking up an idea that was "in the air" at his time and using it to explain the significance of Jesus of Nazareth. Therefore, we are dealing not with a source but rather with parallels. For a more detailed discussion, see R. E. Brown, *The Gospel According to John (I-XII)*, Anchor Bible (Garden City, NY: Doubleday, 1966) pp. 519-532.

What is one to make of all these parallels? None of them needs to be rejected as totally irrelevant. There are good reasons to think that John was deliberately pulling in various religious currents of his time and that here and elsewhere in his Gospel he was trying to make the point that Jesus fulfills and transcends all these currents. With the description of Jesus as the Word of God in the Prologue he may well have been comparing him to the Old Testament word of the Lord, the personification of Wisdom, the Philonic *logos*, the Law, and the Greek philosophical *logos* and suggesting that Jesus is all these and more. But the Jewish texts describing Wisdom as a personal figure are probably to be taken the most seriously among all these parallels. The discovery of the Dead Sea scrolls has shown that the language and thought patterns of Johannine tradition are much more at home in oriental or even Palestinian Judaism than was previously believed. The parallels from Sirach 24, Wisdom, and 1 Enoch 42 are the closest to John 1:1-18 in content and in historical setting, and so these should probably be given pride of place in interpreting the hymn to Jesus as the Word and Wisdom of God.

## *Bibliography: Parallels*

### *Documents in English Translation:*

R.H. Charles (ed.), *The Apocrypha and Pseudepigrapha of the Old Testament in English,* 2 vols. (Oxford: Clarendon Press, 1913).

J.H. Charlesworth (ed.), *The Old Testament Pseudepigrapha* (2 vols.; Garden City, NY: Doubleday, 1983, 1985).

H.F.D. Sparks (ed.), *The Apocryphal Old Testament* (New York: Clarendon Press, 1984).

G.W.E. Nickelsburg, *Jewish Literature Between the Bible and the Mishnah* (Philadelphia: Fortress, 1981).

M.E. Stone (ed.), *Jewish Writings of the Second Temple Period* (Philadelphia: Fortress, 1984).

A. Dupont-Sommer, *The Essene Writings from Qumran* (tr. G. Vermes; Magnolia, MA: Peter Smith, 1971).

T.H. Gaster, *The Dead Sea Scriptures in English* (3rd ed.; Garden City, NY: Doubleday, 1976).

G. Vermes, *The Dead Sea Scrolls in English* (rev. ed.; London: Penguin, 1987).

H. St. J. Thackeray et al., *Josephus,* 9 vols. (Loeb Classical Library; Cambridge, MA: Harvard Press, 1926-65).

F.H. Colson et al., *Philo,* 10 vols and two supplements (Loeb Classical Library; Cambridge, MA: Harvard Press, 1929-62).

H. Danby, *The Mishnah* (Oxford: University Press, 1933).

J. Neusner, *The Mishnah* (New Haven—London: Yale University Press, 1988); *The Tosefta* (New York: Ktav, 1977-86); *The Talmud of the Land of Israel* (Chicago: University of Chicago Press, 1982- ); *The Talmud of Babylonia* (Atlanta: Scholars Press, 1984- ).

C.G. Montefiore and H. Loewe, *A Rabbinic Anthology* (New York: Schocken, 1974).

J.M. Robinson (ed.), *The Nag Hammadi Library* (San Francisco: Harper & Row, 1977).

B. Layton, *The Gnostic Scriptures* (Garden City, NY: Doubleday, 1987).

E. Hennecke, *New Testament Apocrypha* (ed. W. Schneemelcher; tr. R. McL. Wilson; Philadelphia: Westminster, 1963-65).

*Collections of Documents in English:*

C.K. Barrett, *The New Testament Background: Selected Documents* (rev. ed.; London: SPCK, 1987).

H.C. Kee, *The New Testament in Context. Sources and Documents* (Englewood Cliffs, NJ: Prentice-Hall, 1984).

*Jewish History in the Time of Jesus:*

M. Hengel, *Judaism and Hellenism. Studies in their Encounter in Palestine during the Early Hellenistic Period* (tr. J. Bowden; Philadelphia: Fortress, 1974).

*The Jewish People in the First Century* (ed. S. Safrai and M. Stern; Compendia Rerum Iudaicarum ad Novum Testamentum I/1-2; Philadelphia: Fortress, 1974-76).

E. Schürer, *The History of the Jewish People in the Age of Jesus (175 B.C. - A.D. 135)* (rev. and ed. G. Vermes and F. Millar; Edinburgh: Clark, 1973, 1979, 1987).

V. Tcherikover, *Hellenistic Civilization and the Jews* (tr. S. Applebaum; Philadelphia: Jewish Publication Society, 1961).

# 10. THE MEANING OF THE TEXT

## *A. What the Text Says*

THE AIM of exegesis is to explain as far as possible what the text meant to its original audience and in its original historical setting. Because we live in a world and a time quite different from the world of the New Testament, we need to work harder at the exegesis of New Testament texts than we might have to work at understanding a novel written in our own country during the past five or ten years. With the modern novelist we probably share a language, thought patterns, cultural assumptions, and values. Even if our agreement is not total, we do have much in common and probably do not need a third party to explain the novel to us. A noted literary critic once said that no book written in the past one hundred years should need a commentary. His point was not that modern works are simpler than ancient works but that commentaries on ancient writings supply us with precisely the kind of information that intelligent readers of today bring to writings of our own time. We need commentaries on ancient works to tell us what the words meant, what cultural assumptions were current, and what literary conventions were in fashion.

Those who understand and can use the elementary techniques of exegesis are in a position to do some of the work of the commentator on their own. But beginners and even experienced scholars often fall into the habit of rushing to commentaries to resolve difficulties met in the Scriptures without first having made an effort at thinking the text through for themselves. If we wish to penetrate through the words of the New Testament to its meaning, if we believe that the process of understanding these texts can be a creative enterprise, if we assume that the word of Scripture is a living word, then the burden of exegesis is on us. The very use of a commentary can teach us much about exegesis and can furnish helpful guidance, but it is no substitute for our own efforts at understanding and interpreting the text.

In order to grasp what the text says, we must apply the procedures described and illustrated in the previous chapters of this book (see Appendix Two). That can seem like an overwhelming task, but once the habit of asking the right questions is developed the work can be carried out more expeditiously than it may seem at first sight. *Literary criticism* looks at the words of the text and its images and symbols, the characters and their relationships, the progress of thought, the literary form, and the relation of form and content. The other operations described in this book are really specializations within the general process of literary criticism. *Textual criticism* studies the variant readings found in the ancient manuscripts and tries to arrive at the form of the original text. Consulting several reliable *translations* can alert us to the textual problems within the manuscripts, the interpretive decisions facing the translator, and the different philosophies of translation. *Word study* is concerned with the various occurrences of the term in all kinds of texts, the meaning of the term in this particular context, and its place in the term's history. *Source criticism* asks whether the document being studied had a source before it, what the source tried to say, and what was the relationship of the author to the source. *Form criticism* analyzes the literary shape of the text and tries to establish the history of that form. *Historical criticism* focuses on the event behind the text and what can be said about it. *Redaction criticism* considers the unique views and unusual emphases placed upon the sources and the life situation of the redactor and his community. *Literary parallels* to New Testament texts highlight the points of contact and divergence and enable us to understand better the social setting and cultural assumptions of the texts. All these procedures are parts in the process of listening to the text in an effort to grasp what it meant in its original setting. These are the elementary steps in New Testament exegesis.

Nevertheless, few people who read the Scriptures are satisfied with merely determining what the text meant in antiquity. Most of us come to the Scriptures with the assumption that we will find there something significant for the way we live our lives and the way we think about ultimate realities. The church's emphasis on the important place of the Bible within public worship reinforces our expectations that spiritual insight can be found in the Scriptures and that this insight can make a difference in our personal and social lives. But the transfer of spiritual insight from the New Testament to the present is more complex than it may appear at first glance.

## *B. What Others Have Brought to the Text (The History of Interpretation)*

We approach everything with presuppositions. Our family life as children, our education, and our experiences during life all influence the ways in which we react to events and even to literary texts. Exegesis without presuppositions is impossible. The existence of the presuppositions cannot be denied, but awareness of them can allow us to distinguish as effectively as is possible between what the text is saying and what we bring to it.

Before turning to the assumptions that we ourselves bring to the text, perhaps a look at some important moments in the history of biblical interpretation can shed light on the process of grasping and articulating the meaning of biblical texts for our own time. The history of interpretation can also provide some perspective on the methods explained and exemplified in this book and help us to see their strengths and limitations.

In handling the Old Testament Jesus used many of the methods that other Jewish interpreters of his time used. He cited texts from the Old Testament to provide instruction for conducting one's life and for proving theological points. Nevertheless, Jesus did not hesitate to criticize some sayings in Scripture (see Mt 5:21-48), to distinguish between what was from Moses and what was from God (see Mk 10:2-9), and to establish a hierarchy of important truths within the Old Testament (e.g., love of God and love of neighbor take precedence over the strict observance of the sabbath). While acknowledging the authority of the Old Testament Scriptures, Jesus exercised a free and an authoritative attitude toward them. Paul too used the typical Jewish methods of interpretation and accepted the assumptions of Jewish exegesis at most points, but he also brought some specifically Christian presuppositions to the Old Testament. For Paul and for the other New Testament writers as well, Jesus was the promised Messiah. That meant that Jesus Christ provides the key that unlocks the mysteries of the Scriptures, and so Old Testament prophecies and personalities were understood as foreshadowings of Christ. Paul read the Old Testament through the filter of Christ and believed that the true understanding of the Scriptures is a gift from God through the Holy Spirit (see 2 Cor 3:16-18).

The biblical interpretations produced by the Fathers of the Church are frequently divided into the Alexandrian and Antiochean schools. Alexandria in northern Egypt was the great academic center of antiquity. Among the many projects carried out there were the attempt to show the spiritual meaning behind Homer's Iliad and Odyssey and Philo's effort at proving that the truths of the Old Testament do not contradict or differ radically from the highest spiritual insights of Greek philosophy. The greatest Christian representatives of the Alexandrian current of biblical interpretation were Clement of Alexandria and Origen. These interpreters assumed that (1) all Scripture has a spiritual sense, (2) the purpose of Scripture is the revelation of truths, (3) Scripture is to be interpreted by recourse to parallels within Scripture, and (4) allegorical interpretation reveals the hidden meaning. Whatever their faults as interpreters may be, the Alexandrians rescued biblical interpretation from fundamentalism and excessive literalism.

Antioch in Syria was a very early and important center of Christianity (see Gal 2:11), and the major biblical interpreters representing this current of exegesis were Theodore of Mopsuestia and John Chrysostom and to some extent Jerome. More influenced by Aristotelian thought than Platonic thought, this current of biblical interpretation emphasized the historical reality of the biblical revelation and insisted that any higher or deeper sense of Scripture must be based on the literal sense. Their literal and exegetical method of interpretation was very influential and provided the foundation for most modern exegesis.

A third current within patristic exegesis can be labelled as "traditional" or "ecclesiastical." In his struggles with the gnostics in the late second century A.D., Irenaeus of Lyons criticized the gnostic use of Scripture for neglecting the order and the context of the passages and for interpreting the clear and the obvious by the dark and the obscure. As a positive standard of interpretation Irenaeus pointed to the faith as preserved in the churches of the apostolic succession. In the third century Tertullian, a North African, spelled out the matter even more logically. According to him Jesus came to preach the truth of revelation and entrusted it to the apostles, and the apostles in turn transmitted the truth to the churches that they founded. Therefore only the churches that stand in the succession of the apostles possess the teaching of Christ. Vincent of Lerins in the fifth century argued that biblical interpretation must proceed according to the ecclesiastical tradition and reflect what is catholic ("what has been believed everywhere, always, and by all"). The notions of apostolic succession and catholicity reflected in this current of interpretation are full of historical and theological problems, but on the positive side teachers like Irenaeus, Tertullian, and Vincent had a strong and admirable sense of the Bible's place within the life of the Christian community.

The so-called "fourfold sense" of Scripture played an important role in the medieval interpretations of the Bible. Developed from allegorical exegesis, this theory assumed that a text has four levels: literal (what happened), allegorical (the hidden theological meaning), anagogical (the heavenly sense), and moral (the relevance for the individual's behavior). Thus Jerusalem in Gal 4:22-31 is a city in Palestine (literal), the church (allegorical), the heavenly home of us all (anagogical), and the human soul (moral). But Thomas Aquinas insisted that the literal sense must be the basis for all others: "Nothing necessary to faith is contained under the spiritual sense that is not elsewhere put forward by Scripture in its literal sense." He also tried to bring together biblical truth and philosophical truth and used reason as a tool in understanding and explaining the Scriptures.

In his actual interpretation of biblical passages Martin Luther owed much to medieval exegesis, but some of his principles of interpretation were new, at least in their formulation. Proceeding from the less controversial to the more controversial, we may express them in this way: (1) The Scriptures in their basic message about Christ are sufficiently clear for anyone to understand. (2) A historical understanding of the biblical author and his times is essential to exegesis. (3) Scripture as God's word is the criterion by which the church is to be judged, and the church is not the arbiter of Scripture. (4) The fundamental criterion is Christ as seen in the core books of the New Testament (Romans, Galatians, John, 1 Peter).

But the stage for the modern interpretation of Scripture was really set by the rediscovery of classical texts during the Renaissance and the development of methods for editing and interpreting them. These ancient texts showed that, far from arising in a historical vacuum, the Scriptures were very much a part of their times. Another development paving the way for some kinds of modern interpretation was the divorce of philosophy from the Scriptures so that a philosopher like Spinoza could argue that where philosophy and Scripture collide (e.g., on miracles), then Scripture is to be rejected.

The modern way of interpreting the Scriptures is frequently described as the "historical-critical method." As we have already seen in this book, the historical-critical method applies to the Scriptures all the tools that have been found useful in analyzing any piece of literature. It assumes that Scripture was written in a historical setting and must be understood with reference to what the words and ideas meant to people of that period. Before making personal applications, the interpreter must struggle with the meaning of the text in its original setting. According to the historical-critical method, exegesis means first and foremost explaining what the text meant in its original situation. Over the centuries a series of concerns or questions (see Appendix Two) helping us to grasp certain aspects of the text's meaning have been developed, but modern interpretation does not cast aside the concerns and questions of earlier exegetes. The relative importance of the literal sense and whatever other dimensions may be discerned, the place of the Bible within the church, the canon within the canon of Scripture, and the relation between philosophy and Scripture—these issues continue to be debated in the modern study of the Bible. The historical-critical method taken by itself cannot resolve these issues. As generally used today and as described in this book, the historical-critical method is an approach to the literature of the Bible and not a philosophy or a theology. Whatever the claims of its early practitioners and its present-day opponents, the historical-critical method need not be perceived as a threat to Christian faith.

## C. *What We Bring to the Text*

Having seen something of the assumptions that interpreters in the past have brought to the Scriptures, we now should look at the personal, philosophical, and religious presuppositions that we bring to the New Testament text. Descriptive exegesis tries to state what the text said to its original readers. But the very act of description is also a kind of new creation. At the most obvious and fundamental level, the exegesis of a biblical text involves explaining a passage written in Greek most likely by a Jewish-Christian author under the sway of the Hellenistic culture of the Roman empire to a twentieth-century audience of Americans (or whatever other national group) who speak English and live in what is variously described as the post-Enlightenment age or the atomic age. The literary form in which the descriptive exegesis is presented may be a commentary or an article in a scholarly journal and differs radically from that of the original text, which may be a parable or a miracle story or a letter. The concerns of the exegete are objectivity, clarity, logical consistency, and precision in expression—not necessarily the primary concerns of the religious writers in antiquity. The point is that even the most apparently objective and unbiased exegesis necessarily involves translation into a different language, a different literary genre, and a different framework of thought.

The inspection of one's personal presuppositions involves both social and psychological elements. Such an inspection is necessary because interpreters should know and be conscious of the baggage that they bring to the task of biblical interpretation. I am a white American male living in the middle to late twentieth century, born of immigrant parents (from Ireland), raised in the Boston area, the product of parochial schools, a Jesuit now for thirty years, a Roman Catholic priest, a teacher of Scripture in a seminary in Cambridge, MA, holding a doctoral degree in biblical languages from Harvard, and so on. Each and every one of these elements has some impact upon the way I approach a biblical text. Remove one or two of them from my biography and substitute something else, and surely my reading of the text would change. I will spare the reader an inventory of my psychological strengths and weaknesses, but this omission should not be taken as suggesting that the interpreter's psychological predispositions are not important. Good interpreters must know themselves in order to distinguish between the message of the text and the social and psychic interference that they bring to it.

Few of us look upon ourselves as philosophers. But if we give any thought at all to ultimate questions about humanity, the world, God, or ethics, we are indeed philosophers in practice. In the history of interpretation there have been many attempts to "translate" the message of Scripture according to the language and thought-categories of full-blown philosophical systems. For example, the Alexandrian interpreters relied on a form of Neoplatonism, and Thomas Aquinas borrowed much from Aristotle. In our times Rudolf Bultmann has used the existential philosophy of Martin Heidegger to write a theology of the New Testament. Bultmann's use of Heidegger is instructive, because he viewed Heidegger's categories not as the importation of a foreign body into biblical studies but as the modern reflection of the thought-categories of Scripture itself. In other words, there is, according to Bultmann, a genuine correspondence between biblical thought and Heideggerian thought. Though Heidegger was not explicitly a religious philosopher, it is entirely possible that the language and dynamics of religious experience influenced him far more than it is sometimes admitted. Theologians rely on philosophical categories to express the message of Scripture because these categories may be current in some circles and because they may furnish the biblical interpreter with the language and concepts needed for adequately communicating the experiences captured in the biblical texts.

It is at the level of philosophical presuppositions that I would locate the so-called "new methods" of exegesis. Liberation interpretation begins with the experience of the poor and/or women and aims to open up the "subversive" texts of the Bible through and for the political engagement of Christians. It seeks to regain the original function of the Scriptures as life-texts for the oppressed. This orientation is concerned with the social classes and interests represented by the actors in the text, the point of contention or struggle, the way in which the conflict is resolved, and the present-day sociological analogies. Psychoanalytic interpretation naturally owes much to Sigmund Freud and Carl Jung and explores the basic human desires expressed in the biblical texts. For example, why is the parable of the prodigal son in Lk 15:11-32 so attractive to so many people? It may be because in that parable (according to Freudian analysis) the father as the ego attempts to satisfy the demands of both the younger son as the id and the older son as the superego. Or it may be because (according to the Jungian analysis) the parable involves the alienation of the ego (the prodigal son) from the self (the father) and its reintegration through coming to terms with the shadow (the older son). Relying upon the linguistic research of Ferdinand de Saussure and the anthropological theories of Claude Levi-Strauss, structuralism is concerned with the operation of signs within a structural system, how these signs reciprocally condition one another, and how an underlying code determines the range of possibilities within which the signs operate. This method explores the semantic oppositions operative in human thought and in the structure of reality itself. All three of these new methods go beyond (or ignore, according to their critics) the strictly historical task of exegesis and try to explore how much modern sociological, psychological, and semiotic insights can contribute to our appreciation of the texts of the Bible.

Besides the personal and philosophical presuppositions that we bring to the biblical text, we also bring religious presuppositions. The Scriptures are a collection of religious texts, and practically all of us come to them in search of religious insight. Most readers of the Bible belong to a church and so tend to read the New Testament within the social and intellectual framework of a particular faith community. For most of us, biblical exegesis is not simply an exercise in studying ancient texts under all possible aspects and with all available resources. Biblical exegesis carried on within the church is primarily interested in the content, transmission, and present-day relevance of the text's message. It appeals to faith and tries to show how the biblical author can guide the reader toward life with God in his kingdom. This kind of "ecclesiastical" exegesis runs the risk of dogmatism, pietism, and mystification. Nevertheless, the church in which we live out our religious lives assumes that the biblical texts read in public worship shed light on human experience today. That light is traditionally uncovered in preaching, and this domain of activity provides the specific illustrations for this chapter. The controversy about the great commandment in Mt 22:34-40 and the exhortation to suffering Christians in 1 Peter 4:12-16 have been chosen precisely because both texts touch upon the differences between ancient consciousness and modern consciousness and so illustrate the task of trying to articulate publicly the meaning of a biblical text for today.

## *D. What It Means Today (Preaching on Biblical Texts)*

1. *Matthew 22:34-40 (Preliminary Observations):* In the outline of Matthew's Gospel the passage about "the great commandment in the law" occurs in a block of four controversies or debates with the Pharisees and Sadducees about paying taxes to Caesar (22:15-22), the resurrection of the dead (22:23-33), the great commandment (22:34-40), and the identity of the Messiah (22:41-46). The block appears after Jesus' triumphal entry into Jerusalem (21:1-11) and before the passion and resurrection narrative (26—28). It aims to provide sample material to explain what got Jesus' opponents so angry as to have him killed. Therefore Mt 22:34-40 is one element in a block of debates in which Jesus gets the better of his opponents.

The passage has parallels in Mk 12:28-34 and Lk 10:25-28, but the precise relationship between the three texts is not entirely clear. The discrepancy has been explained in a variety of ways: (1) Matthew has rewritten Mark very extensively. (2) Matthew had access to the Q version of the story, though Luke differs radically from it. (3) Matthew had access to another tradition. (4) Matthew freely composed the text on his own with little attention to sources. So varied are the options that it is best to approach this text on its own grounds with little attention to Synoptic relationships:

> [34]But when the Pharisees heard that he had silenced the Sadducees, they came together. [35]And one of them, a lawyer, asked him a question, to test him. [36]"Teacher, which is the great commandment in the law?" [37]And he said to him, "You shall love the Lord your God with all your heart, and with all your soul, and with all your mind. [38]This is the great and first commandment. [39]And a second is like it, You shall love your neighbor as yourself. [40]On these two commandments depend all the law and the prophets."

There are a few basic points of information that the reader ought to know about this passage. The Pharisees were a lay religious movement active in Jesus' time that took the exact fulfillment of the Law as their ideal and expressed their fellowship in community meals. The lawyer mentioned in Mt 22:35 was a Pharisee who was skilled in the interpretation of the Old Testament and the traditions surrounding it. The request to summarize the teaching of the whole Law in a single sentence was a task often set before Jewish teachers in Jesus' time. When Hillel (a contemporary of Jesus) was asked to summarize the Law while standing on one foot, his response was this: "What you hate for yourself, do not do to your neighbor. This is the whole Law; the rest is commentary. Go and learn." Jesus' answer in vv.37-39 combines Deuteronomy 6:5 and Leviticus 19:18. He insists that both love of God and love of neighbor be present but does not say that they are the same thing. The image underlying the word "depend" in v.40 is that of a large mass hanging on the thread of the two commandments. The Pharisees were the great religious rivals of Matthew's community, and so in Mt 22:34-40 Jesus gives a distinctive response to a typically Pharisaic question.

The following is a homily on Mt 22:34-40 preached to a community in a parish church in a suburb of Boston. It provides much more exegetical information than is usual or necessary in homilies, but this group seems to be quite interested in such matters. I present it here primarily because it touches on issues that distinguish the concerns of people in Jesus' time from those of our own time and because it raises some very interesting questions of interpretation.

*Love of God and Love of Neighbor (Mt 22:34-40):* "On these two commandments depend all the law and the prophets." In the Scripture reading from Matthew's Gospel we have a statement of what is often taken as the core of Jesus' teaching—the commands to love God and to love our neighbor. Jesus' contemporaries had counted up the number of laws in the Old Testament and had distinguished 613 different commandments. These laws covered all areas of life, and trying to keep track of them was not easy. So the great teachers of the day attempted to enunciate some statement that would serve as a summary of all the laws. One great teacher was even challenged to summarize the whole law while standing on one foot. Obviously, his reply would have to be brief. Jesus' statement in today's Scripture reading represents his attempt at summarizing the whole Law.

What is the content of Jesus' summary? What does he say? In forming his summary, Jesus quotes two passages from the Old Testament. One that says: "You shall love the Lord your God with all your heart, and with all your soul, and with all your mind." The other says: "You shall love your neighbor as yourself." With these words of Scripture, with these words that would have been familiar to his hearers, Jesus says that all the laws, all the religious experience of Israel, indeed all the religious aspirations of the human race come down to two things: love of God and love of neighbor.

It is important to notice that while Jesus was asked to state the greatest commandment of the Law, his reply consists of two commandments—love of God and love of neighbor. He makes very clear that the two are not the same thing, that they can and should be considered separately. It is a delusion to substitute love of God for love of neighbor, and a delusion to substitute love of neighbor for love of God. Yet the fact remains that anyone who says he loves God and hates his neighbor, that person is a liar. The very fact that Jesus cites two commandments rather than one in his reply means that, even though love of God and love of neighbor are not the same things, they cannot exist apart from one another.

What did Jesus mean by the commandment to love God? Well, it would mean acknowledging God as creator and Lord. It would mean praying to him in a spirit of faith and truth. It would mean acting in ways that are appropriate for one who takes God seriously, especially in ways that are in accord with Jesus' own teaching. What did Jesus mean by the commandment to love one's neighbor? It would mean that we are to look on our fellow human beings as creatures of God, as brought into existence by him and sustained in life by him, as loved by God. It would mean that we can and should go beyond the artificial limits imposed by social status, sex, or race. Lastly, it means taking very seriously that part of the commandment that says "as yourself." "You shall love your neighbor *as yourself*." Each of us has a natural instinct for self-preservation and self-protection. If we had no self love at all, we could not get through the day in one piece. By this saying ("love your neighbor *as yourself*") we are being challenged to consider showing the same quality of care and concern for other people as we do so naturally for ourselves. By this saying we are urged to put away our selfishness and to open our hearts to others.

"You shall love the Lord your God . . . You shall love your neighbor as yourself." The words are so familiar to us that their very familiarity can obscure their meaning and blunt the challenge implicit in them. Yet if Jesus thought enough of them to consider them an adequate summary of the whole religious history of his people, should we not make a genuine effort to explore what they might mean in our own lives? Should we not ask ourselves daily how we stand with respect to the words: "You shall love the Lord your God . . . You shall love your neighbor as yourself?"

*Concluding Observations:* In preaching based on the Scriptures one works on the level of "post-critical naiveté." That is, having wrestled with the meaning of the passage and its genesis (sources, context, content, form, historical setting, etc.), the preacher tries to put the text back together again and to say what it meant for its original audience and what it may mean today. The homily on Mt 22:34-40 presented here is not very revolutionary, but it does seek to avoid some of the pitfalls of preaching on this passage. The first pitfall is to turn this text (and indeed every text in Scripture) into a moral lesson or an allegory of the soul and not to pay attention to the framework in which the text appears in Scripture—the controversy between the Pharisees and the disciples of Jesus as to who constitutes the people of God. Another pitfall avoided here is to insist on this text as demonstrating Jesus' originality when in fact he is answering a standard question with the two quotations from the Old Testament. The combination of the two quotations may be unique but the material in them is traditional. A third pitfall is to use the stress on the presence of both love of God and love of neighbor to combine the two into one thing, to say that love of neighbor equals love of God. That may be an attractive theory to some people, but the text of Mt 22:34-40 seems to go out of its way not to identify the two commandments (see v.39). Though inseparable, love of God and love of neighbor are not the same.

But by far the most tempting modern pitfall is to overemphasize the phrase "as yourself" in the quotation from Lev 19:18 in v.39: "You shall love your neighbor as yourself." Twentieth-century psychology has uncovered the existence of much personal ambivalence about the self and has shown that one cannot love someone else unless one first loves oneself. This may well be an important and urgent psychological truth, but in the biblical tradition self-love is an assumption and is not being explored at all in this text. The point of Mt 22:39 is this: Assuming that we naturally and instinctively love ourselves at least enough to feed and protect ourselves, we are challenged to make a similar effort at loving others. The text is not really interested in the issue raised in modern psychology. This is not to say that preachers cannot talk about the need for self-esteem. It only means that preachers should not put forward Mt 22:34-40 as a passage concerned with self-esteem when in fact it deals with love of God and love of neighbor as distinct but inseparable.

2. *1 Peter 4:12-16:* 1 Peter is a gem among the New Testament writings. Written to and for Gentile Christians in Asia Minor at some time between A.D. 70 and 90, this document explores the difference that Christianity could make in the lives of a tiny minority movement in a sea of paganism. 1 Peter 4:12-16 furnishes advice for these Christians in their sufferings and provides a good opportunity to compare the social settings of a first-century church in Asia Minor and of a twentieth-century church at least in the Boston area:

> [12]Beloved, do not be surprised at the fiery ordeal which comes upon you to prove you, as though something strange were happening to you. [13]But rejoice in so far as you share Christ's sufferings, that you may also rejoice and be glad when his glory is revealed. [14]If you are reproached for the name of Christ, you are blessed, because the spirit of glory and of God rests upon you. [15]But let none of you suffer as a murderer, or a thief, or a wrongdoer, or a mischief-maker; [16]yet if one suffers as a Christian, let him not be ashamed, but under that name let him glorify God.

*Ancient and Modern Christianity (1 Peter 4:12-16):* "If one suffers as a Christian, let him not be ashamed, but under that name let him glorify God." In the course of this series of homilies on the first letter of Peter, I have often drawn attention to the social situation of the Christians to whom the letter was written. As a small and apparently insignificant group they were suffering misunderstanding and perhaps even persecution. But far from succumbing to self-doubt and despair, these Christians took consolation from the example of the suffering Christ and courageously endured what came their way. Their consciences were clear, and that fact enabled them to put up with opposition and force. In today's reading several of these perspectives are reinforced: the Christians are to remain hopeful in their sufferings; they are to avoid all evil doing; and they are to glory in being thought worthy to suffer as Christians. In all their tribulations these people were confident that being Christians was an important and positive thing. They were convinced that their good deeds and good example would win others to Christ; their missionary strategy placed more emphasis on good deeds than on words. They were convinced that being Christians was an exciting and joyful adventure, not a burden to be ashamed of.

Most of us here came to Christianity by a different route from the people to whom this letter was first written. They chose Christianity whereas we were born into it. We live in a very different society. They were a tiny movement in a pagan world whereas we live in a nation where the majority is at least nominally Christian. Nevertheless, being Christians in twentieth-century America is just as challenging and just as important as it was in the first-century A.D.

We may live in what is called a Christian country, but there are many assumptions floating around in our society and in our world that are directly opposed to Christian faith and need to be challenged by it. There is the assumption that human beings can be explained solely in biological terms and are just another species of the animal kingdom. There is the assumption that there are no ultimates in life and that only the *how* is important, not the *why*. There is the assumption that all the great works of the human spirit—art, literature, religion—can be reduced to class conflicts or primitive urges. There is the assumption that the world is the great arena of competition and that the survival of the fittest is all that matters. Personal comfort, instantaneous gratification, self-love—these seem to be the prevailing values of the culture that comes through to us on television, in movies, and in books. Put in these terms, this modern ideology is far from the true Christian faith. In the face of scientific positivism, Christianity teaches that each human being is a child of God and created for eternal life with him. In the face of moral and spiritual relativism, Christianity insists that we have been created to praise, reverence, and serve God and that this constitutes the goal or purpose of our lives. In the face of reductionism, Christianity encourages and celebrates the great achievements of the human spirit. In the face of competition, Christianity teaches us to love one another, care for one another, and share with one another. As Christians we can endure suffering patiently and put aside selfishness.

This comparison of the assumptions of modern ideology and those of Christian faith shows us very graphically the choice that is before us. As I said before, it is just as challenging and just as important today as it was in the first century A.D. to make the effort to be genuine Christians. Furthermore, our world sorely needs genuine Christians—people who call into question its easy assumptions and show that another way is both possible and preferable. May we work at being Christians and rejoice to be called by that name! May we imitate the example of the Christians in the first century!

*Concluding Observations:* This text and the homily on it are fairly clear and need little explanation. The homily aims to give people a sense of the social situation implied by the biblical text and tries to develop the differences and the similarities between it and their own situation. It seeks to show that in many ways Christians today are as much a cognitive minority as they were in the first century A.D.

Perhaps a few words on the relationship between preaching and prayer are in order at this point. Preaching in the church is a public action that must respect the unique character of each biblical text and the faith of the Christian community. Therefore preachers have a serious obligation to listen to the word of Scripture first and foremost and then bring to it the insights of personal experience and prayer. I make this point because all too often homilies are impressionistic ("it strikes me") or the occasions for preachers to get off their pet theories and personal prejudices. Preachers have no right to pass over the preliminary operations of biblical exegesis and to substitute their own "wisdom" for the traditions of Christian faith. Prayer over the scriptural text may well be a necessary step prior to preaching, but it should not be confused with the rational process of exegesis that is necessary if the public character of preaching is to be respected. On the other hand, exegesis may purify one's private prayer and put it on paths that are healthy and faithful to the Christian tradition. Nevertheless, it is no substitute for personal encounter with God in prayer.

## *E. Exegesis and Spirituality*

In the previous section I cautioned against confusing exegesis and prayer and against supposing that, if the biblical passage inspires me with a fruitful movement of the soul, the meaning of the text has been discovered. I was primarily concerned with preaching as a public activity within the church, but my remarks may have sounded as if I was criticizing or even belittling personal prayer. Nothing could be further from the truth! I sincerely believe in the importance of personal prayer and practice it myself on a regular basis. Here I would like to explore more explicitly some aspects of the relationship between the exegetical methods outlined and illustrated in this book and personal spirituality.

Spirituality is the style of the person's response to the grace of God in the challenges of everyday life. Defined in this way, spirituality is a personal and unique affair—the way in which God encounters me and I encounter God. But as human beings and as Christians we are also part of a people, and so our spirituality necessarily includes a communal dimension. There are even schools of spirituality (Benedictine, Franciscan, Dominican, Ignatian, etc.), which offer hallowed methods of participating in and expressing our Christian faith. Spirituality as a stance before God encompasses all dimensions of the human person, but it reaches a peak moment in the personal conversation with God that we call prayer. Prayer is personal encounter with God, while exegesis is the rational analysis of a literary text. Obviously they are not the same thing. Nevertheless, biblical exegesis can open up new directions in personal prayer by clarifying for us the kinds of religious experience that our community holds up as models; e.g., Abraham, Moses, Isaiah, Jeremiah, Jesus, and Paul. Furthermore, if our religious experiences have some connection with the directions and thrusts of the biblical tradition, we know that at least they stand in a line intelligible to and approved by the Christian community. In other words, biblical exegesis can serve as a partial guarantee that our personal spiritualities are not outside the boundaries of the Christian tradition and the Christian community. It supplies one (among several) objective criterion for assessing a personal spirituality.

Many schools of spirituality encourage the use of a biblical text as the starting point for prayer. Surely God can lead the individual in whatever direction he chooses, and surely prayer involves the imagination and emotions of the person in addition to the rational faculties. Granting these most important facts, I do think that some general guidelines can be laid down regarding the use of Scripture in prayer: (1) In prayer one operates on the level of post-critical naiveté; that is, having wrestled with the meaning of the text and its genesis (source, form, redaction, etc.), one puts it back together as a whole and tries to say what it means now. (2) The literal meaning of the text must be respected. The principle enunciated by the Fathers of the Church that any "spiritual" meaning must have a basis in the literal sense is still sound. The Scriptures should not be used as something on which we can hang our fantasies. (3) Not every passage in Scripture is suitable for prayer. Some sections were not written at all with prayer in mind, and those who use Scripture in prayer must be sensitive to this fact. On the other hand, the Psalms with their wide variety of religious themes and their ability to engage both heart and mind constitute an extraordinary school of prayer on their own. (4) Redaction criticism with its emphasis on the perspective of the final biblical author can be especially helpful in praying over the Scriptures. In this way we can place ourselves beside the writer and try to look at Christ in the same way that he did. Furthermore, when scriptural prayer is done on a regular basis, it can be very helpful to focus on a single portrait of Jesus (Matthew's, John's, Paul's) and to explore the many aspects of it. (5) We must avoid reducing every biblical text to the "individual" level. In fact, the Bible is seldom concerned with individual psychology. To reduce Jesus' parables of the kingdom of God to allegories of our individual psyches is to block out the message of Scripture and to substitute our own truncated variety of religion for it. An effort should be made to remain faithful to the social framework in which the texts of Scripture were written and to try to broaden out the scope of our prayer and get more in touch with social realities.

How are exegesis and spirituality related? Biblical exegesis as the methodical analysis of a religious text should enrich and refine our spirituality and thus help our prayer. As the study of the sacred texts of our religion, it puts us in touch with the authentic Christian tradition and furnishes a kind of objective criterion for evaluating religious claims. The way in which one engages in prayer depends largely on the unique dispositions of the person who is praying, but anyone who claims that his or her prayer arises from the Scriptures must try to understand those Scriptures, respect their literal meaning, and stand beside the biblical writers in their efforts at grasping and articulating the ways of God in human existence.

## *Bibliography: Interpretation*

E. Best, *From Text to Sermon. Responsible Use of the New Testament in Preaching* (Atlanta: John Knox, 1978).

R.E. Brown, *Biblical Exegesis and Church Doctrine* (New York—Mahwah, NJ: Paulist, 1985); *The Critical Meaning of the Bible* (1981).

*The Cambridge History of the Bible,* 3 vols. (Cambridge: Cambridge University Press, 1963, 1969, 1970).

R.M. Grant and D. Tracy, *A Short History of the Interpretation of the Bible* (Philadelphia: Fortress, 1984).

K. Hagen et al., *The Bible in the Churches. How Different Christians Interpret the Scriptures* (New York—Mahwah, NJ: Paulist, 1985).

E. Krentz, *The Historical-Critical Method* (Guides to Biblical Scholarship; Philadelphia: Fortress, 1975).

W.G. Kümmel, *Introduction to the New Testament* (tr. H.C. Kee; Nashville/New York: Abingdon, 1975).

W.G. Kümmel, *The New Testament: The History of the Investigation of Its Problems* (tr. S. McL. Gilmour and H.C. Kee; Nashville/New York: Abingdon, 1972).

B.J. Malina, *Christian Origins and Cultural Anthropology* (Atlanta: John Knox, 1986).

I .H. Marshall (ed.), *New Testament Interpretation. Essays on Principles and Methods* (Grand Rapids, Eerdmans, 1977).

S. Neill, *The Interpretation of the New Testament 1861-1961* (New York: Oxford, 1964).

D. Nineham, *The Use and Abuse of the Bible. A Study of the Bible in an Age of Rapid Cultural Change* (New York: Barnes & Noble/Harper & Row, 1977).

E. Schüssler Fiorenza, *Bread Not Stone. The Challenge of Feminist Biblical Interpretation* (Boston: Beacon, 1984); *In Memory of Her. A Feminist Theological Reconstruction of Christian Origins* (New York: Crossroad, 1983).

A.C. Thiselton, *The Two Horizons* (Grand Rapids: Eerdmans, 1980).

## *Appendix One: The Dating of the New Testament Books*

Most of the individual volumes in the series entitled "The New Testament Message" include brief discussions of the traditional questions of introduction (authorship, place of composition, audience, date, etc.). But it may be useful here to list the dates attributed to the various documents in the two most comprehensive and authoritative German introductions to the New Testament: W. G. Kümmel's *Einleitung in das Neue Testament* (Heidelberg: Quelle & Meyer, 1973) and J. Schmid's thoroughgoing revision of A. Wikenhauser's *Einleitung in das Neue Testament* (Freiburg —Vienna: Herder, 1973). The remarkable agreement between these standard reference works shows that the differences between the critical Protestant scholarship represented by Kümmel and the critical Catholic scholarship represented by Schmid are no longer very great. All the books except Paul's epistles are assigned dates after A.D. 70. Those "Pauline" epistles dated to a time after 70 (Ephesians, 1 and 2 Timothy, Titus) are considered to have been written in Paul's name but some time after his death in the early sixties of the first century.

| **Book** | **Kümmel** | **Schmid** |
|---|---|---|
| Matthew | 80-100 | 80-90 |
| Mark | ca. 70 | ca. 70 |
| Luke | 70-90 | 80-90 |
| John | 90-100 | 90-100 |
| Acts | 80-90 (or 100) | 80-90 |
| Romans | 55-56 | 58 |

| | | |
|---|---|---|
| 1 Corinthians | 54-55 | 57 |
| 2 Corinthians | 55-56 | ? |
| Galatians | 54-55 | 54-58 |
| Ephesians | 80-100 | ca. 90 |
| Philippians | 53-55 or 56-58 | ? |
| Colossians | 56-58 or 58-60 | 58-60 or 62-63 |
| 1 Thessalonians | 50 | 51-52 |
| 2 Thessalonians | 50-51 | 51-52 |
| 1 Timothy | 100-110 | ca. 100 |
| 2 Timothy | 100-110 | ca. 100 |
| Titus | 100-110 | ca. 100 |
| Philemon | 56-58 or 58-60 | 58-60 or 61-62 |
| Hebrews | 80-90 | 80-90 |
| James | ca. 90-100 | ca. 90-100 |
| 1 Peter | 90-95 | after 70 |
| 2 Peter | 125-150 | 120 |
| 1 John | 90-110 | 90-100 |
| 2 John | 90-110 | 90-100 |
| 3 John | 90-110 | 90-100 |
| Jude | 100-110 | ca. 100 |
| Revelation | 90-95 | 90-95 |

This whole reconstruction has been vigorously challenged by J. A. T. Robinson in *Redating the New Testament* (Philadelphia: Westminster, 1976), who argues that all the New Testament writings were composed between A.D. 47-48 (James) and 68 (Revelation) and that the fifties of the first century represented the most creative period in the primitive church's activity. But that book should be read along with two important review articles that opt for the Kummel/Wikenhauser-Schmid position in its general outlines: D. M. Smith, Jr., "Redating the New Testament?" *Duke Divinity School Review* 42 (1977) 193-205 and J. A. Fitzmyer, "Two Views of New Testament Interpretation: Popular and Technical," *Interpretation* 32 (1978) 309-313.

## *Appendix Two: Questions in Exegesis*

1. *Literary Criticism in General*

What words, images, and symbols appear?
What characters appear, and what are their relationships?
What is the progress of thought?
What literary form does the text have?
How does the form contribute to expressing the content?

2. *Textual Criticism*

Are there ancient variant readings?
What can be explained away as unconscious or conscious alterations?
What reading is demanded by the context, language, and style of the document?

3. *Modern Translations*

What Greek text underlies the translation?
What decisions did the translators have to make?
What philosophy of translation is operative?
Has anything been lost in translation?

4. *Word Study*

Where else does the word appear, and what does it mean there?
What meaning does it have in this context?
Where does this instance stand in the term's history?

5. *Source Criticism*

Did the document being studied have a source?
What did that source say?
How has the author used the source?

6. *Form Criticism*

What is the literary form of the text?
What does the literary form tell about the history of the community?

7. *Historical Criticism*

What really happened?

8. *Redaction Criticism*

What unique views or unusual emphases does the author place on the sources?
What is the author's life situation and theological outlook?

9. *Parallels*

What elements do the two texts have in common, and at what points do they differ or contradict one another?
What is the historical relationship between the two texts?

10. *Meaning (Hermeneutics)*

What does the text say?
What do we bring to the text?
What does it mean today?

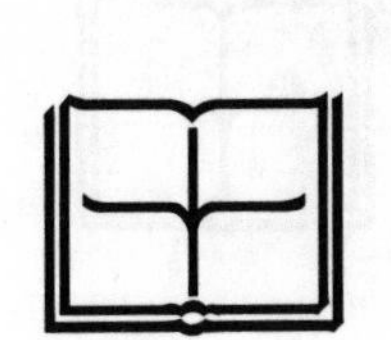

# NEW TESTAMENT MESSAGE

*A Biblical-Theological Commentary*

Wilfrid Harrington, O.P. and Donald Senior, C.P.
EDITORS

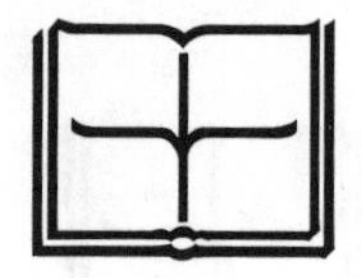

*New Testament Message, Volume 1*